BASIC HANDBOOK ON
MENTAL ILLNESS

BASIC HANDBOOK ON

Mental Illness

HARRY MILT

CHARLES SCRIBNER'S SONS
New York

Copyright © 1974, 1973, 1971, 1965 Harry Milt

Library of Congress Cataloging in Publication Data

Milt, Harry.
  Basic handbook on mental illness.

  1. Mental illness. I. Title. II. Title: Mental
illness. [DNLM: 1. Mental disorders. WM100
M662b 1974]
RC454.M4956 1974   616.8'9   73–19278
ISBN 0–684–13738–0
ISBN 0–684–13753–4 (pbk.)

This book published simultaneously in the
United States of America and in Canada—
Copyright under the Berne Convention

All rights reserved. No part of this book
may be reproduced in any form without the
permission of Charles Scribner's Sons.

1 3 5 7 9 11 13 15 17 19   C/C   20 18 16 14 12 10 8 6 4 2

Printed in the United States of America

Contents

Contents

Foreword

Throughout history, as far back as ancient Greece, madness was attributed to possession by deities, demons, or witches. Only at the turn of the twentieth century did we begin to see the influence of biological science on our understanding of mental illness, and to witness the systematization of this new knowledge, first in Emil Kraepelin's classification of mental disorders and then in the monumental work of Sigmund Freud who rationalized the mysterious workings of the mind in an essentially biological framework, providing, for the first time, a comprehensive theory by which humanity could begin to understand itself.

Finally, a science emerged which wed psyche to soma and brought medical and psychological knowledge into an integrated system for the study and treatment of abnormal behavior. Psychiatry finds its application, today, not only in treatment, but also in such diverse fields as law, criminology, education, child development, geriatrics, city planning, international relations, even space travel. As it moves into these areas, it is faced with the task of explaining complex concepts to those without special training. Fortunately, a solution is being found in the work of medical writers, people who have both scientific knowledge and the blessed talent to translate it into clear, understandable prose.

The work of Harry Milt is outstanding in this field. I became acquainted with him when I was President of the American Psychiatric Association and he was Director of Public Information of the National Association for Mental Health. In our work together, I was greatly impressed with his capabilities not only as a communicator but also as a student of theory. In my review of his *Basic Handbook on Alcoholism* I expressed admiration for the skill with which he worked through a morass of punitive nonsense to provide a masterly, objective overview of this subject.

Later I read with equal admiration his *Basic Handbook on Mental Illness*, finding it a remarkably lucid, simple, yet comprehensive and scientifically excellent presentation. I was not at all surprised, therefore, when the book found ever-growing use for training in mental health centers, mental hospitals, schools of nursing, colleges, high schools, and with the new allied health professions. At the Mayo Clinic it has been in use for several years.

I am delighted that the book is now being published by Charles Scribner's Sons in an expanded, up-to-date edition and I am confident it will have widespread use for many more years, not only by the professions, but also as a personal reference book for laymen.

HOWARD P. ROME, M.D.
Senior Consultant, Psychiatry, Mayo Clinic,
Rochester, Minnesota; Past President,
American Psychiatric Association; and
President, World Psychiatric Association

Preface

People coming into the mental health field today may find it difficult to believe that a generation or so ago the subject of mental illness was taboo in the press and broadcast media and that community mental health services were virtually nonexistent.

Today, mental illness is discussed openly and freely everywhere, and very few would question the proposition that a person with a mental illness is a sick person in need of care, treatment, and rehabilitation. Nearly every community has mental health services available to it in mental health clinics and centers, general hospitals, family service agencies, public health facilities, welfare facilities, group health agencies, or through colleges, churches, and trade unions. Several of the emerging new health professions are related to personnel needs in the mental health field. Thousands of citizens are becoming involved as volunteers in hospitals, clinics, and centers. Public mental health education, once the exclusive province of mental health associations, has become a major undertaking of many facilities.

An inevitable outgrowth of this great upsurge has been the growing need for basic information about the different mental and emotional disorders, their causes, their symptoms, the methods by which they are treated, the places where they are treated, and the professionals involved in treatment.

As Director of Public Information of the National Association for Mental Health, I often wished in vain that someone would put all this information together in one place. Finally I decided to do it myself.

It did not take long for me to realize what a difficult task I had undertaken. I was concerned not only that the information be comprehensive, sound, and scientifically accurate; I also wanted it to be equally meaningful and useful to the many different audiences for which it was intended: professionals, college and high school students, and the interested layman.

To approximate this ideal as closely as possible I depended on the guidance of professionals in all branches of the mental health field. I wish to express my infinite gratitude to the following people who were generous enough to give me their suggestions and comments and to give the handbook their enthusiastic endorsement: Francis J. Braceland, M.D., editor, American Journal of Psychiatry; C. A. Hardin Branch, M.D., former president of the American Psychiatric Association; S. T. Ginsberg, M.D., medical director of several Veterans Administration psychiatric hospitals and formerly mental health commissioner of the state of Indiana; Daniel L. Lieberman, M.D., formerly commissioner of mental health in Delaware and California; William Malamud, M.D., director emeritus of research and medical services, National Association for Mental Health; and C. J. Ruilmann, M.D., formerly director of mental health and hospitals for the state of Texas.

BASIC HANDBOOK ON
MENTAL ILLNESS

CHAPTER ONE

What Mental Illness Is

Illness is any condition which causes the body, or any part of it, to perform in an abnormal way.

In indigestion, it is the stomach or intestines which perform abnormally; in pulmonary tuberculosis, the lungs; in high blood pressure, the circulatory system.

In mental illness, the abnormality is in the mind and emotions and overall behavior. It results in the kind of behavior that causes others to say "He is not in his right mind" or "There is something wrong with the way he acts."

The abnormality is indicated by three basic types of behavior: unrealistic, irrational, and inappropriate.

There are many different kinds of mental illness resulting from many different kinds of causes. It would be more accurate to speak of "the mental illnesses" than of "mental illness," since the term refers to a collection of different disorders arising from many different causes, having in common only the characteristic that they are abnormal.

Here are some illustrations of mentally sick behavior:

A girl suffers from extreme feelings of inferiority, thinks that no one likes her, finds it difficult to make and keep friends, and has frequent spells of melancholy.

A man is continually restless and tense, given to frequent outbursts of extreme anger with very little cause, and has migraine headaches.

A mother suffers a continuous, painful anxiety that she is going to die of cancer. When that anxiety fades, she has others, such as unfounded worries about financial security, about danger to her children, about fires in her home.

A college student suffers an intense attack of paralyzing panic every time he goes into a crowded room.

A girl falls into a semistupor, remaining that way week after week, unable to recognize her relatives, babbling and laughing to herself.

A young man says his insides are made of glass and that "secret rays" and voices are controlling him and making him do things.

A man rushes into traffic, hurls himself to the ground, and pleads with the drivers to run over him because he is "evil and needs to be punished."

These examples demonstrate that mental illnesses, like physical illnesses, range from mild and barely recognizable to severe and obvious. No one would hesitate to say that the man in the last example is mentally ill. People in other periods of history—and unfortunately even some people in our own age—would simply dismiss him as "crazy." But the girl in the first example has feelings that everybody experiences at some time or other, and she might therefore not even be recognized by her family or friends as ill.

The terms mental illness and mentally ill are relatively new. They came into being when medical science discovered that the strange, abnormal things mentally sick people do are symptoms of underlying illness, an illness of the mind and emotions.

The belief that one's insides are made of glass, the sitting in a stupor and babbling, the panic in a crowded room, the anxiety about dying of cancer, the tenseness and migraine headaches, the spells of melancholy are all symptoms of mental illness, in the way a fever and a cough are symptoms of physical illness.

The observable mental, emotional, and behavioral symptoms are only part of the illness—the external part. There are also abnormalities in the internal machinery of the mind and emotions—the nervous system, glands, circulatory system, and the physical, chemical, and physiological processes through which these systems operate.

The mind and emotions do not exist apart from the body.

It is impossible to think a thought, have an idea, or experience a feeling without the involvement and participation of the body. For every thought that goes on in the mind there is an electrical and chemical process going on in millions of nerve fibers in the brain. For every feeling of happiness or sadness or fear or disappointment there are chemical and physical processes going on in the brain, in the autonomic nervous system, in the glands, in the bloodstream, in the respiratory system, and in the digestive system.

We think and feel not only with our minds but with our bodies. When something is wrong with a person's mind or emotions, something is also wrong in the functioning of the bodily processes.

The fact that both the mind and the body are involved in the manifestation of mental illness does not necessarily indicate the cause of mental illness (whether the cause is "physical" or "mental"). It indicates only that mental illness involves both the body and the mind.

Causes

There is no single answer to the question, Is the cause of mental illness mental or physical? There are many kinds of mental illness, some having physical causes, some predominantly mental causes, and some a combination of the two.

Mental illnesses in which the cause is known to be entirely physical are those resulting from injury to brain tissue caused by a wound or by infectious diseases such as syphilis, meningitis, or encephalitis. Many symptoms of the mental disorders resulting from such injuries are indistinguishable from symptoms occurring in mental disorders believed to be primarily psychological or mental in origin.

There are other mental illnesses presumed to have primarily a physical cause—not in the form of injury to nerve tissue, but in the form of inborn constitutional abnormalities or defects which prevent normal emotional development (in the way that certain inborn constitutional abnormalities prevent normal intellectual development and result in mental deficiency). An example is primary infantile autism, a mental illness in which the child fails to grow out of the isolation, remoteness, and nonresponsiveness of the first few months of childhood. Such children act as though they are living in a shell, unaware of the real world around them and unresponsive to people and surroundings.

The great majority of mental illnesses, however, are believed to have a predominantly psychological cause—

stressful emotional experiences in childhood that warp the normal emotional responses and cause the individual to behave abnormally.

Even this concept, the concept of the predominance of psychological influences, makes allowances for physical influences too. Many psychiatrists believe that the children who develop abnormal emotional responses as a result of stressful emotional experiences in infancy are already somewhat defective to start with—that they are born with a constitutional defect that makes them unable to handle stress the way normal children do.

That is the prevailing theory, for example, about schizophrenia, the most widespread of the psychoses (serious mental illnesses). People who develop schizophrenia are believed to have an inherited vulnerability which makes them especially sensitive to parental rejection and punishment, or which makes them perceive as rejection or punishment what other children might perceive as ordinary inattention. Signs of emotional distress are apparent in these children early in childhood. Later in life, especially during adolescence, severe emotional stress is apt to produce a complete breakdown.

In the mental illnesses known as the neuroses, the cause is believed to be almost entirely psychological. Rejection or excessive punishment by the mother—or overindulgence and overprotection—are believed to hold the child at infantile stages of emotional behavior and in a constant state of turmoil throughout life. Yet, even in the neuroses, some psychiatrists believe, there must be some constitutional defect, some inherited weakness which makes some children more vulnerable than others to the supposedly detrimental influences of the mother.

Whether the basic cause is psychological or physical or a combination, the result is a personality marked by abnormal behavior. The abnormality may be manifested continuously, or only from time to time. The situation in which the individual finds himself and the people with whom he interacts may play an important part in triggering the onset of illness. This is especially true in cases where the original cause was essentially psychological and where the present situation confronts the individual with the same type of stress or danger which caused the formation of the abnormal pattern of response to start with.

For example, there are some children who develop a deep dependency relationship with the mother. If they feel the mother's love and affection, constantly and continually, then everything is all right. But if there should be any hint that the mother does not love them or like them, they feel terribly threatened. This may produce an abnormal reaction—symptoms such as anxiety, depression, or physical illnesses. Formed in early childhood, this abnormal response pattern remains in a latent state, ready to emerge whenever the child, and later the adult, is confronted with a threat to the dependency relationship. This may happen, in childhood, when a new baby (and rival) is born, when the child starts school, or when the mother is sick, or away. In such instances, the vulnerable child feels he is being abandoned, and he reacts with the abnormal patterns formed in infancy.

Later in life he may transfer the dependency relationship to a teacher, a good friend, an employer, or his mate, and react with an abnormal response (mental illness) when the relationship with this person is threatened.

Interpersonal relationships, therefore, play a very important part in the development of mental illnesses—as an original cause in the formation of the abnormal response and as a contributing factor later on.

Much has been said about the importance of social and economic factors in producing mental illness, factors such as poor housing, slum conditions, and poverty. These are generally considered to be secondary, contributing causes, rather than primary causes. For example, a mother plagued by poverty, illness, hardship, and a miserable relationship with a drunken and improvident husband is likely to vent her own resentment, impatience, hostility, frustration, and anger on a child born into this situation. Instead of the protection, affection, guidance, and supervision the child needs for healthy emotional development, he may be subjected to scolding, beating, dislike, and rejection. Even an ordinarily healthy child, and especially one with extreme sensitivity or vulnerability, will respond to this situation with disturbed behavior.

Aged people who are displaced from a setting of social and economic importance and usefulness are more likely to develop symptoms of mental disorder than those who continue in an active, productive setting in which they have a place and an important role.

Hence, psychiatry is concerning itself today not only with the correction and control of basic causes but also with the secondary and contributing factors in the social and economic environment.

Major Classifications of Mental Illness

A great deal is known about mental illness in general, but there is still a long way to go in identifying and naming the different specific mental illnesses. The classifications of mental illness are still quite broad—not at all as precise as the classifications of the physical illnesses. The psychoses and the neuroses are two major classes of mental illness. Within the broad category of neurosis are listed such illnesses as anxiety neurosis, obsessive-compulsive neurosis, and the phobias. Under psychosis are listed such illnesses as schizophrenia, manic depressive psychosis, involutional psychoses, and organic psychosis. But not one of these individual illnesses is nearly as precise in its identification and symptom picture as is pneumonia, tuberculosis, coronary thrombosis, appendicitis, or any of the other well-known physical illnesses.

While there is some difference among psychiatrists as to classification of mental disorders, psychiatry departments in medical schools break them down, for teaching purposes, into a number of major classes:

Psychoneurotic disorders (neuroses)
Psychotic disorders (psychoses)
Psychophysiological disorders (psychosomatic illness)
Personality disorders
Disorders caused by injury to brain tissue or impairment of brain tissue function such as head wounds, encephalitis, syphilis, chronic alcoholism, pellagra.

This book is chiefly concerned with the first four classes.

CHAPTER TWO

Neuroses
and How They Develop

Like all mental illnesses, the neuroses are marked by thoughts, emotions, and behavior that are irrational, unrealistic, and inappropriate to the situation.

In the neuroses—as compared with the more serious mental illnesses known as the psychoses—these aberrations are moderate rather than extreme. They occur intermittently rather than continually. Months, even years, can go by in which there is hardly any evidence of trouble, and then, in an emotionally difficult and painful situation, the neuroses breaks out in an acute form, persisting until the stress is relieved or until the personality has worked out for itself some other adjustment, some other way of reacting to the painful situation.

When they do occur, neurotic disorders occur within a personality that is, for the most part, healthy and in fairly good functioning order, overall. They do not take over and dominate the entire personality, rendering it entirely incapable of functioning in a normal setting.

In his irrational and unrealistic thoughts and behavior, the neurotic person twists, distorts, and gives false meaning to what he hears and sees. He misinterprets reality, but he does not replace it, as does the psychotic person, with his own internal imaginary thoughts and ideas, making these the reality instead of the real world around him. The neurotic person is generally aware that there is something wrong with him. The psychotic person does not; for him, the fantasy is the reality.

The neurotic person may feel sometimes, or even persistently, that he is inadequate or inferior, and he may shun human contact to avoid the pain of an imagined rebuff; but he does not feel utterly worthless, nor does he feel inadequacy with such intensity as to want to kill himself because of it, or to believe that someone is planning to kill him because he is worthless.

He may feel hostile toward other people because of an imagined belief that they do not like him, but he will not go about injuring or killing them as his "enemies."

The neurotic person may experience a severe and even continuing anxiety about his health or job or ability, but the anxiety is not severe enough to paralyze him, to disorganize his thinking processes, and to throw him into fantasy, delusions, and hallucinations.

He may suffer occasional and deep spells of depression or melancholy, but he does "snap out" of them. The spells are not so overpowering as to incapacitate him totally and completely, throwing him into a continued, stuporous state for months and even years.

He may have an exaggerated notion about his ability, power, or importance, but he will not think he is Einstein, the president, or God.

The neurotic person may have daydreams in which he dramatizes his fears, his hopes, his hates, his loves. In his daydreams, he actually "says" things to other people and he has them "saying" things to him, but his daydreams vanish and his mind goes back to the real people and things about him. His daydreams and fantasies never become the reality for him as they do for a psychotic person.

There are a number of fairly distinct types of neurotic conditions or illnesses, each distinguished by a predominant symptom picture, or "reaction." The American Psychiatric Association lists six such major symptom-pictures or reactions: anxiety reaction, depressive reaction, phobic reaction, obsessive-compulsive reaction, conversion reaction, and dissociative reaction.

These are discussed in Chapter 3. To understand them better, it will be helpful to have an explanation of how the neuroses develop (according to prevailing theory).

The human infant is essentially an uncivilized animal with primitive biological needs and desires. He has very strong instinctive urges to eat, to satisfy his natural functions, to sleep, to be warm. He needs to assert himself, to have his way. He has a strong need to be protected against hurt. The most powerful instinct of all is the instinct for survival. This is expressed by the child's attachment to the mother. With the protection of the mother, he feels safe. Without it, he feels the primitive terror of extinction. This attachment must be maintained at all costs; the child feels reassured that it is being maintained when he feels his mother's love.

The mother, however, is not only a source of love and protection, but also a source of control and denial. The child must be weaned, toilet trained, broken of unruly and destructive behavior, of greediness and selfishness for things which give him pleasure. When he is curbed and deprived, he becomes angry, screams, bites, has tantrums, and hates his mother (a primitive, self-protective reaction). This creates a dangerous situation for him. His screaming and raging may cause his mother to stop loving him, and if she does, he cannot survive. Thus, the child is caught in a crucial conflict. How he deals with it depends on three things:

First is the child's capacity to tolerate emotional pain and fear. Children differ in respect to this trait as they do in respect to other emotional (and physical) characteristics. Some can handle distress easily; others "fall apart."

Second is the extent of the child's need for very close emotional ties with the mother. In this respect, too, children differ greatly. There are some children who have an inordinate need for this kind of maternal protection. Others can get along with less.

Third is the mother's own emotional state and her ability to help the child through this difficult period without excessive anger, punishment, and dislike.

The child who has a high tolerance for fear and pain, who has an ordinary or normal need for close ties with his mother, and who has a mother who will help him through this period without antagonism stands the best chance to grow up without neurosis. Others, who are handicapped with respect to one or more of the three conditions, will be unable to resolve the conflict and will need to find an unsatisfactory compromise which, at best, holds the conflict at bay. This compromise solution is the neurotic response.

One child might attempt the solution of becoming outwardly sweet, compliant, and "good," pushing back and swallowing his hate and anger. This is a bid to keep the mother's love and protection at all costs.

Other children are paralyzed by the dilemma and just "freeze," becoming passive and unresponsive. Others find the reality much too painful to endure and, instead of finding a compromise way out through a "strategy," sink into excessive

24

daydreaming, where they can find a fantasy gratification of their needs and a fantasy expression of their antagonism for their mother.

Others turn away from the parent as a source of gratification and turn to themselves as the main source, becoming self-centered and narcissistic and finding their freedom from pain in self-admiration and self-love.

Others are unable to find even such compromise solutions and continue to be angry and aggressive, suspicious and fearful, continuing to express such emotions even though this brings them additional rejection. They find internal solace through self-pity and feelings of hurt.

It is in this way that there are founded the "problem" personality traits in neurotic children and adults—the suspicious, hostile, defensive, angry person; the quiet, shy, self-effacing, withdrawn person; the ultrasweet, always good and eager-to-please person; the selfish, self-centered, narcissistic person who concentrates his efforts on being attractive and winning attention without any interest in true and deep feelings; the ultracritical, self-righteous person who is very strongly for or against something much of the time.

These problem personality patterns, formed in childhood, persist throughout life, achieving no more in adult life than they did in childhood, keeping the person constantly at odds with himself and with others, and continuing to persist no matter how much unhappiness, pain, and discomfort they cause.

The psychiatric term for this fixedness and inflexibility is *rigidity,* and this is the essential feature of the neurotic response. Shaped in the early years, the neurotic response continues to operate in an inflexible, unchanging way, year after year, no matter what the situation. Because it is related to something that happened in the past, it is bound to produce behavior that is not in accordance with the present reality, that makes little sense in terms of present conditions, and that is inappropriate to the present situation—the basic characteristics of mentally sick behavior.

The problem personality trait is only one part of the neurotic response. Another part is the neurotic symptom.

As the child attempts to work out a compromise solution to his dilemma, he must fight back the powerful emotions of craving, anger, resentment, and fear that are causing the impossible conflict. They cannot just be ignored and forgotten. The only thing that can be done with them is to repress them—to keep them out of direct expression. But repressing them does not end them. So long as the basic conflict remains unresolved, the emotions continue to be generated and to operate forcefully through indirect, disguised expression. This indirect, disguised expression is the mental or physical symptom.

Among the mental symptoms of neurosis are anxiety, depression, phobia, and obsessive thoughts and acts. Among the physical symptoms are migraine headaches, indigestion, loss of appetite, tic (muscle twitch), allergies, and chronic fatigue.

There is still a third part to the neurotic response—the persistent craving for satisfaction of the unsatisfied need.

The original frustrated need may have been for closeness to the mother; this, in later life, might be carried on as an urgent need to be very close to people. It may have been for continued helpless dependence upon the mother, and this might be carried on in later life as an insistence on having everyone else do things for him, and a refusal to accept responsibility. It may have been for independence and freedom from excessive punishment, control, and discipline; this might be expressed in adult life by the inability to yield to warm, close relationships for fear of being dominated and controlled.

A very strange and basic aspect of this continued craving is that it is insatiable and will persist even though later life provides that which was earlier denied. The man who craves closeness to people will seek out people who will give it to him—like friends or a wife. Yet this closeness will do little to satisfy a need that persists in its infantile state. A person whose frustrated craving is for self-assertiveness will seek it through the acquisition of power or importance, but the continued acquisition of these will do little to relieve the original need that persists in its infantile state. A person whose frustrated craving is for freedom from control may attempt to fulfill it by staying single or by divorcing one mate after another, yet he will never experience the freedom internally.

In neurosis, a device which was created to deal with an unbearable problem in childhood continues to operate throughout life in spite of the fact that it does nothing for the individual except to cause him unhappiness and pain.

In some cases, the neurotic response is triggered off because someone or something in the current situation resembles a key aspect of the original situation. In others, the neurotic response appears to require only that the situation contain a general threat to the person's sense of self-esteem or emotional security.

CHAPTER THREE

Neurotic Reactions

Anxiety

Anxiety is a sense of apprehension that something unpleasant or harmful is going to happen. In normal people and under normal circumstances, it is a normal response. If a person knows that there is a personnel cutback coming in his plant, he is anxious that he may be one of those to be dismissed. If a neighbor's child comes down with encephalitis, a mother becomes anxious that her child might have been infected, too. In normal anxiety, there is a probable cause.

But in neurotic anxiety, there is either no real cause for the anxiety, or a very slight cause which is highly exaggerated, bringing on an intense, entirely inappropriate anxiety response.

If the baby is sick with a cold, the neurotic parent may

imagine that this is the beginning of pneumonia. If he himself has a stomachache, or if he has a pain in the chest, he imagines he is having a heart attack. If a new person comes on the job in the office, he thinks this person has been hired to replace him.

The anxiety may take the form of a constant preoccupation with health, the imagining of all kinds of symptoms (hypochondria), the running from one doctor to another. Or it may not be attached to any specific person or situation at all, taking the form of a free-floating anxiety, a vague, tormenting feeling that something bad is going to happen.

Anxiety is often accompanied by a feeling of tension, irritability, and restlessness. Frequently it is also accompanied by a variety of physical symptoms such as indigestion, headaches, constipation, difficulty in swallowing, tension pains in the back of the neck, chronic fatigue, loss of appetite, excessive appetite, dizziness, palpitations, and difficulties in sexual response.

It is important to remember that anxiety is a symptom and that a symptom is an indirect or disguised expression of a repressed, unacceptable emotion. The more the repressed emotion is in danger of coming into consciousness in recognizable form, the greater is the anxiety. An attempt to understand the anxiety and deal with it in terms of the present situation will be only partially successful.

The same is true of the physical symptoms that accompany anxiety. They, too, are indirect or disguised outlets for repressed emotions. It is useless, therefore, to attempt to talk someone out of his anxiety by proving to him there is no real justification for it; such an attempt just will not work. The anxiety is not amenable to reason. A person experiencing a neurotic anxiety about cancer, for example, may go to a specialist, undergo every kind of test, and be reassured by the physician that nothing is wrong with him; but the anxiety will inevitably return or be replaced by another one.

Depression

Depression in a mild form, the feeling of dejection, is a normal response accompanying a disheartening disappointment, failure, or loss. It is a part of the grief and woe that is experienced at the departure or loss of a loved one. Normally, this feeling wears itself out as other concerns and preoccupations crowd back in.

In neurotic depression, the feeling of dejection either comes without any apparent cause or is entirely out of proportion to it. Accompanying the depression there is often a heightened irritability and sensitivity—a tendency to feel abused and "put upon."

In some types of neurotic depression there is a feeling of being "bad," of being unloved, of being a failure. In others, there is just a decreased interest in living, a loss of enjoyment of anything, a dispirited feeling.

Depression is frequently accompanied by bodily complaints such as headaches, fatigue, tightness of the head, loss of appetite, constipation, insomnia, and loss of weight.

The depressive reaction may come in an acute, intense form lasting for hours, dissipating only with a change in the immediate situation. Or it may persist as a continued, dull, nagging, gray mood.

Since depression, like anxiety, is a symptom, it may be regarded as the indirect expression of a repressed emotion, generally that of anger and resentment which the individual does not dare to express lest they bring on retaliatory punishment. Such depression may carry with it a feeling of hopelessness.

Phobias

A phobia is an unreasonable, exaggerated fear of a specific object or situation. Agoraphobia, for example, is a fear of open spaces. A person suffering from agoraphobia dreads leaving the house to venture out in the street unless accompanied by another person. He may fear that he will suffer a heart attack, faint, or come to harm in some other way, or the fear may be vague and undefined. This dread may keep a person homebound for years.

Another common phobia is claustrophobia, the fear of enclosed places. A person suffering from this phobia is unable to remain in a closed-in area like a room, elevator, auto, subway train, or theater without experiencing a feeling of panic. The condition is relieved somewhat if there is a door nearby which the victim knows he can use if he has the impulse to leave suddenly. An anxiety that one may fall down in a faint or cry out uncontrollably is also experienced in claustrophobia.

Acrophobia is a fear of high places. The victim experiences a fear that he may fall or jump from the height.

Other common phobias are unreasonable revulsion for or fear of animals, such as cats, dogs, birds, or mice.

The theoretical explanation of phobias is that they represent a detachment of a repressed emotion from its original object and a disguised attachment to some other unrelated object or situation. Thus, the original emotion might have been hate for or horror of the parent. This socially unpermissible emotion becomes intolerable for the child, and so he represses it. But repression does not end it and it continues to be generated in one disguised form or another—sometimes as anxiety, sometimes as a depression, sometimes as a phobia.

Obsessive-Compulsive Reaction

One method the mind uses to keep a repressed thought or emotion from coming into consciousness is to occupy itself with a repetitively obsessive thought. A similar method is the compulsive act—a ritual which must be carried out over and over again in a set way. While the obsessive thought or compulsive act may be troubling to the point of distraction, or even to the point of interfering with normal functioning, conscious efforts to escape from the thought or act are of no avail, since they are operated by psychological mechanisms outside conscious control (in the same way that the pumping of the heart or flow of gastric juices operate independently of conscious control).

The compulsive act may take any one of a thousand different forms. It may consist of touching a hand to different parts of the body repetitively in a fixed order. It may involve arranging things on a desk or in a room in a definite, minutely worked-out pattern. Deviation from the fixed order or pattern causes intense anxiety, even panic.

Compulsive behavior is very commonly associated with fear of dirt, uncleanliness, or germs. Every object that is touched is "contaminating"; therefore, it is necessary to wash the hands over and over again. All sorts of devices are developed to avoid touching things, such as opening the door with elbows or gloves. In one case, a patient went so far as to go about on roller skates while cleaning the house in order not to become soiled.

The person apt to show obsessive-compulsive rather than other neurotic symptoms is one whose personality might be described as rigid—strict, stubborn, inflexible, intolerant, overconscientious, and highly critical of others.

Conversion

Occasionally a patient comes to a physician or a hospital with a sudden and unexplainable blindness, deafness, muteness, paralysis of an arm or leg, loss of the sensation of taste or smell, or loss of sensation in an area of the skin.

When careful examination and tests fail to reveal any organic cause for the disorder, the diagnosis very often turns out to be conversion reaction, a psychological disorder.

In conversion reaction (formerly called hysterical conversion), as in other neurotic symptoms, a forbidden, repressed emotion finds an indirect outlet through the disabling of a sensory or motor function of the body. The sensory functions are those of hearing, sight, taste, smell, and touch. The motor functions are the use of the arms, legs, vocal cords, tongue, and other musculature which is normally under voluntary control.

The term conversion has reference to the fact that an emotion, which is an experience of the mind and feelings, is converted into a bodily symptom.

Another kind of conversion reaction is the uncontrollable twitch or spasm affecting muscles of the face or limbs; still another is the experiencing of imaginary symptoms of illness to the point of actually feeling the aches and pains.

Conversion reactions are generally recognized by the fact that the patient shows an unnatural lack of concern about the disability. They seem to occur most frequently in relation to a frightening or threatening event of the present (although the predisposition to the development of this symptom arises out of experiences of the past). They occur especially in connection with traumatic situations such as combat, a holdup, an auto accident; or in connection with an emotionally taxing situation such as sexual conflict; or a situation demanding a demonstration of competence, strength, ability, or judgment.

People most prone to this type of neurotic symptom are of a personality type characterized as immature and narcissistic, self-indulgent and self-centered.

Dissociation

Another form of neurotic reaction which occurs in connection with acutely painful emotional episodes is the dissociative reaction. The term dissociative means that a whole section of mental and emotional life is dissociated from—separated from—the main operation of a total personality. Sometimes it is merely blocked out of the mainstream of consciousness; sometimes it sets up an independent existence of its own, apart from the mainstream of conscious life.

The most commonly known dissociative reactions are somnambulism and amnesia.

In somnambulism (sleepwalking), the person gets up during his sleep and walks about. He is half in a dream state, half in a waking state. His eyes are open and he is in contact with and aware of his surroundings, but only as though they are part of his dream. He may respond if someone talks to him, but what he says will be related to what he is thinking in his dream. The split-off, dissociated "dream state" dominates the personality, obscuring the waking personality's awareness of and relatedness to his external surroundings.

In amnesia, the person forgets who he is or where he comes from. His intimate and personal relatedness to his immediate surroundings is blocked out—dissociated. He will be able to react normally to people as people and to the ordinary events which make up the content of daily life, but he will have no recognition of, or memory for, the people or events which are part of his intimate, personal life. Sometimes the amnesia is partial, blocking out memory of just some individual person, some individual event, or some limited time period. In extreme cases, a large part of the person's previous life or all of his previous life are blocked out. When amnesia occurs, it comes generally after an intolerably, unendurably painful episode, the memory of which must be blotted out.

A rare but highly dramatic type of dissociative reaction is the multiple personality of the kind illustrated in *Dr. Jekyll and Mr. Hyde* and *The Three Faces of Eve.* In multiple personality it is as though a number of entirely different people were occupying the same body, taking over at different times.

CHAPTER FOUR

Psychoses

The psychoses are a large group of mental illnesses characterized by severe disturbances of thought and emotion. (The psychoses were formerly known as "insanity.") Within this group are a number of distinct mental illnesses, each with its own symptom patterns and course of development.

While the disturbances in thought, emotions, and behavior are extreme in the psychoses, amounting to what is descriptively known as derangement, it should be understood that the nature, extent, and duration of the derangement vary from one mental illness to another, and even from one stage to another of the same illness.

In advanced stages of certain types of psychoses the derangement is so complete that the patient might as well be living in another world. Hour after hour, day after day, week after week, year after year, he sits or lies in one position, unheeding, unresponsive to his surroundings, little more than a human vegetable. In other kinds of advanced psychosis, the patient will sit and talk to himself, or walk around talking to unseen people and hearing nonexistent voices, making strange motions with his hands and weird grimaces with his face, acting as though he were living entirely inside himself, entirely unaware of the world and the people outside; this will go on day after day and month after month.

On the other hand, there are cases in which the person looks normal, acts normally, knows who he is and where he is, and is not recognizable as psychotic until he begins to express thoughts about his "insides being made of glass" or about "the secret rays that are coming from the radio" and controlling his thoughts, or about the "plot by the FBI and the president" to keep him imprisoned. In such cases, the disturbance is not spread over every aspect of functioning. It is limited to the chain of delusional thoughts (false ideas about himself and the intent of others), but these are so extreme and bizarre as to distort his other thinking processes and interfere with his relations to other people.

There will be differences in the extent and nature of the disturbances from one stage of the illness to another. In an acute, agitated stage of psychosis the person may seem completely deranged—thrashing about, screaming, talking wildly and irrationally, hearing voices, failing to recognize relatives and friends. But several days later—or even several hours later—the same person may be sitting quietly and docilely talking to a relative, knowing to whom he is talking.

Schizophrenia

In terms of frequency of cases schizophrenia is the most common psychosis. The word means "disintegrated personality"—not "split personality."

Instead of functioning as a coordinated, harmonious, integrated personality with thoughts, emotions, and behavior operating as a purposeful whole, the person exhibits bits and pieces of unconnected, unrelated, disharmonious, irrational functioning without purpose, direction, or design. Thoughts and ideas become distorted, irrational, and bizarre; they are expressed in confused, meaningless, strange language, or nonsensical sounds; or they are not expressed at all and there is only silence. Relationships with other people fade away as the mind turns inward. Emotions become distorted, exaggerated, confused, and inappropriate. Behavior becomes strange, meaningless, and purposeless.

Psychiatrists are not certain whether schizophrenia is one disease with a number of different types, each type characterized by a distinctive symptom picture, or whether there are, in fact, many different diseases classed together under this one heading only because they have the common characteristic of the disintegrated personality. Some psychiatrists speak of "the schizophrenias" rather than "schizophrenia."

Most cases of schizophrenia have their onset during adolescence and early adult life; a small percentage between the thirties and middle age.

The first signs of schizophrenia show up many years before the actual breakdown. In this early stage, there are a number of tendencies toward withdrawal. There is evidence of abnormal sensitivity to "hurt," of feeling unloved, rejected, unworthy. There follows a loneliness, moodiness, suspiciousness, separation from others, aloofness, unresponsiveness. Other early symptoms include a preoccupation with internal thoughts and feelings—giving an impression of being far away—and a lessening of attention to the family, school, work, personal appearance, responsibility, and normal habits and activities. Strong, lusty, live emotional responses begin to disappear, to be replaced by flat, shallow, shadowy emotional responses. There is no longer any excitement—one way or another—about anything. Instead, there is a drifting, listless unresponsiveness. Irritability and tenseness are the only evident emotions.

Then come a number of "peculiar" responses. The person becomes suspicious that other people are watching and conspiring against him (delusions). There is a preoccupation with physical condition and an obsessive concern with diet and other ways of building oneself up. There is often an abnormal preoccupation with abstract ideas about creation, life, good, evil, God, and religion.

These responses occur in the "incubation" stage; then comes the actual onset, or manifestation of the full-blown illness. There is a depletion and disorganization of the emotions. Either there is no emotional expression at all—total apathy—or whatever there is of it doesn't make sense. There is silly smiling, laughing about nothing.

Another symptom of advanced schizophrenia is depersonalization. The patient has feelings of vagueness, of detachment from everyday reality. He observes himself as though he were somebody else; he can no longer conceive of himself as "I." He may believe that certain parts of his body do not belong to him, that he has no body at all, that he is dead.

Thoughts and ideas become disconnected and lose their meaning. Things are said which are irrelevant, irrational, and illogical; often they are just garbled, unrelated words and sounds, sometimes called "word salad." Sometimes there is a parrotlike repetition of one word or phrase over and over and over again.

Often, even where there is still some meaning left in the things the schizophrenic patient does or says and when the thoughts and ideas are coherent, it is likely that they are delusional in nature (false and exaggerated ideas about the patient himself and the intent of others).

Another symptom of advanced schizophrenia is hallucinations, the seeing, hearing, feeling of nonexistent beings or objects. When a schizophrenic patient talks aloud to someone, that "someone" is actually there in the mind of the schizophrenic. When he says someone is talking to him, he actually hears the voice and accepts it as reality.

Bizarre and meaningless physical activity is another symptom of schizophrenia. The patient may sit or lie in one position for hours, days, and years. He may assume the pose of a statue for hours and days. He may walk around and around, or up and back and up and back within the room or hall, without letup, hour after hour. He may twist up his face in set grimaces or move parts of it in a fixed, repetitive pattern.

Types of Schizophrenia

Simple. The simple type of schizophrenia is marked by a persistent, continuous loss of interest, attention, concern, awareness, responsiveness, responsibility, and purpose. The key emotion seems to be indifference. The personality seems to wither away, and just enough seems to be left to keep the person going on a minimum basis of responsiveness to life and the people, events, and obligations which make up living. Hallucinations and delusions are rare. Social aberrations are common (vagrancy, prostitution, delinquency). On hospitalization, this type of patient continues to maintain a limited, ineffective, and unimpressive contact with his surroundings.

Hebephrenic. The hebephrenic type is characterized by silly, incongruous, and inappropriate smiling and laughter, scatterings of hallucinations, and fragments of delusional thought (rather than complete symptoms of delusional ideas). Thoughts and ideas are fragmentary. Speech is disconnected, incoherent, and illogical. Personal habits of order, cleanliness, and sanitation deteriorate. Grimacing and bizarre mannerisms and posturing are ever present. Response to the surroundings is just about nil, separation from reality nearly complete, and deterioration of the personality very far advanced.

Catatonic. The characterizing symptoms of the catatonic type have to do with motion. In one phase, catatonic stupor, there is little or no motion at all. In the other phase, catatonic excitement, there is excessive, uncontrolled movement and activity. The patient may persist in one phase for long periods or pass quickly from one phase to the other.

In catatonic stupor, the patient remains mute, stuporous, and in one fixed position for long periods of time. His face takes on a masklike quality and his body a statuelike quality. He refuses to move, dress, or eat. While appearing to be in a trance, the patient actually does register what is going on about him.

In catatonic excitement, there is an aggressive, hostile thrashing about and destructiveness. Clothing is torn, objects smashed, people attacked. Hallucinations and delusions are common, as are grimacing, posturing, and wild and meaningless speech. Antagonism, resentment, and negativism prevail. Often there is a refusal to sleep or eat to the point of utter physical depletion and exhaustion.

Paranoid. The basic characteristics of the paranoid type are delusions of persecution (people are out to "get" the patient, to capture him, poison him, kill him) and hostile, aggressive behavior in "defense" against the imagined persecution. There are frequent hallucinations in which voices accuse the patient of wicked actions or thoughts. The patient talks about magical rays or powers or forces which control him. He is frequently assaultive and may be violent. Thoughts and feelings become progressively more disconnected, irrational, illogical, and disorganized.

Childhood Schizophrenia

While adult schizophrenia has been known for a century, it was not until about 1940 that psychiatry gave recognition to the existence of a fairly well-defined group of severe mental illnesses of childhood, considered psychotic because of their severity and persistence, and characterized as schizophrenic because of the similarity of some of the symptoms to some symptoms of adult schizophrenia.

One of the reasons for the delay in identifying this group of childhood mental illnesses is that many of the symptoms are found in other conditions, such as mental retardation and brain damage.

Psychiatry has already identified two distinct types of childhood schizophrenia—primary infantile autism and symbiotic infantile psychosis.

During the first three months of life, the normal child goes through a stage in which he is relatively unaware of the things and people around him and unresponsive to them. This stage passes, and the child soon becomes responsive to sights, sounds, and people.

The child suffering from primary infantile autism (the autistic child) never grows out of the state of isolation and separation. He remains unresponsive to his mother. He does not cuddle or cling. He is out of touch with his surroundings and appears to be living inside a film or shell. There is marked delay in speech and sometimes the child never learns to talk. He is slow and late in learning to crawl or walk. He does not play with other children, is not aware they are around. He prefers to play with inanimate objects, and his play consists of going through repetitive mechanical acts with a toy or other physical object, hour after hour.

The child suffering from symbiotic infantile psychosis is in many ways the very opposite of the autistic child. Not only is he *not* unaware of his mother; he cannot bear to be out of her sight. As he clings to her, it appears to the observer that his body actually melts into hers as though they were one. It is said that this child actually feels himself to be part of his mother and does not ever, in his own mind, fully separate himself from her or think of himself as a separate individual.

The symbiotic child does maintain contact with other people, but it is a one-sided relationship. He demands a great deal of affection, but he does not give any. He is apt to be quite talkative and articulate, but his talk is generally fantastic and full of fear and anxiety. He is given to uncontrollable bursts of anger and destructive activity.

While autistic and symbiotic schizophrenia are two distinct types, there is frequently an overlapping, with the major symptoms of both types found in the same child at different times.

A number of other unusual behavior patterns are characteristic of schizophrenic children. In their early years, these children are often preoccupied with stacking blocks or placing them next to one another for long periods of time, sometimes for hours. They have unusual and extreme interest in spinning toys, such as tops and wheels, and in round objects. They also have a much greater interest in boats and water sports than do other children. Once the schizophrenic child has established a play pattern, it is difficult to change it.

Many of these children have a special interest in climbing up on tables or other objects and jumping off, much more so than do normal children. Some of them have the habit of walking on their toes a good deal of the time; others frequently slap their heads or otherwise beat themselves without apparently feeling any pain. Some whirl themselves around in circles spontaneously.

Manic-Depressive Psychosis

There are many mental disorders in which the personality remains relatively well organized, even though there is extreme disturbance of thought and emotions. One is manic-depressive psychosis, which, as the name implies, consists of opposite emotional states—depression and mania. Depression, as already described, is a state of extreme dejection. Mania is the opposite. It is characterized by excitement, elation, agitation, and hyperactivity. In the typical case of manic-depressive psychosis, there is an alternation between the two phases. The alternation may be quite sudden and frequent, or one phase may persist for a long time before giving way to the other. In many cases, phases may be separated by long periods of normality, and the succession may be that of two or more depressive phases or manic phases before there is alternation with the opposite phase.

In the manic phase, the patient is filled with excitement, enthusiasm, boundless energy. He has a thousand ideas a minute and must tell them to everyone. There isn't anything he cannot do, any problem he cannot solve. The most complex and difficult problems seem to him to be utterly simple and he sees the answers with an unbelievable clarity. He has fantastically exaggerated notions about his power and ability. He has grandiose solutions for poverty, unequal distribution of wealth, war, and disease. He is under terrible internal pressure to bring about great changes and reforms, and if his friends and relatives fail to see the wisdom of his scheme and refuse to go along with him, he sees them as enemies and traitors. He writes letters, dozens of pages long, to officials telling them what he thinks. Much of the time he is in a state of elation. He will sleep very little and yet show no fatigue; hurt and bruise himself and pay no attention to his injuries.

In the depressive state, the condition ranges between mild, continued dispiritedness and dejection, to deep, stuporous depression. In the milder states, the patient has spells of melancholy in which he loses zest for living, feels lack of confidence in himself, loses initiative, and withdraws from activity and responsibility. Every task is burdensome. Worries, doubts, and fears are numerous. There is gloominess, irritability, indecision, oversensitivity, moroseness, and isolation from social contact.

In intense depression, the initial dejection and downheartedness pass into intense emotional distress. The entire physical attitude and posture are those of hopelessness, desperation, despondency, and painful endurance of life. There is an almost total withdrawal of interest and responsiveness to people, the world, and life in general. There is often a sense of terrible dread, a sense of impending disaster. There are frequently attempts at suicide and occasional violence against other people.

Depression

Even though most mental illness may be traced back to some predisposing or preconditioning factor or weakness—either inborn, environmental, or a combination of the two—it should be understood that even healthy, well-adjusted personalities can break down.

We often see people "going to pieces" under conditions of

great emotional stress—extreme and torturous pain, illness, grief, poverty, great fright, or extreme and relentless pressure of work or responsibility. Normally a person will bounce back as soon as the condition is relieved or some adjustment made which allows respite from the particular pressure or emotional pain, or after natural healing processes enable the individual to get over the shock or the painful incident. However, when stress is piled on top of stress, and when there is no respite, no relief, month after month and year after year, even a healthy person can go "out of his mind."

This is what happens in the psychotic condition known as depressive reaction. The person goes into deep, prolonged spells of dejection, hopelessness, confusion, inactivity, dispiritedness, and anxiety. There are feelings of being evil, worthless, in need of punishment. Sometimes there are persecutory delusions. Very often there are thoughts of suicide and, occasionally, suicidal attempts.

Involutional Psychosis

Some psychotic disorders appear to be definitely connected with the involutional period of life—the time, during middle age, when physical, mental, and emotional expansion and growth reach a peak and start to decline. In women, definite and radical glandular changes take place in menopause; other physiological changes, not quite so pronounced, take place in men. But there is reason to believe that the involutional psychotic reaction is more related to the psychological stresses of middle age rather than to the organic changes. The loss of important biological functions (childbearing), the decline of other functions (sexual interest and responsiveness), the fear of the end of life and the inevitable movement toward death—all these tend to act on existing emotional insecurities and weaknesses and precipitate, in some people, the onset of psychotic illness.

There are two types of involutional psychotic reactions, one dominated by depression, the other by paranoid ideas.

Involutional depressive reaction (sometimes called involutional melancholia) is an active, agitated depression filled with anxiety, dread, and agitation rather than the stuporous, immobile dejection found in other depressive states. The patient is given to weeping and moaning. There is an intense feeling of guilt, or worthlessness, of having spent a useless life, of having injured other people, of having committed unpardonable sins and of needing to be punished. The patient "knows" he is going to be destroyed and insists he deserves it. There are also persistent emphasis on imaginary illnesses and fantastic ideas about "the stomach drying up" or the intestines being "shut off from the mouth," as well as refusal to take food and frequent attempts at suicide.

In involutional paranoid reaction, the patient is fearful, tense, and agitated, but not depressed. He thinks evil of others, not himself. He is full of delusional, persecutory ideas. People are trying to poison him or kill him. He thinks that the doctors and nurses are part of an organization plotting to persecute him and make him do unpleasant things, to operate on him, or to give him a disease.

Psychoses of Old Age

There are two types of psychosis associated with old age and believed to be related to organic changes taking place. One of these is called psychosis with cerebral arteriosclerosis. The other is called senile psychosis.

The first is believed to result from changes in the arteries of the brain (the suspected change is that of atherosclerosis, or narrowing of the arterial tube by growing deposits on the wall of the artery, rather than arteriosclerosis, or hardening of the arteries). The other, senile psychosis, is believed to result from general deterioration of the neurological and glandular systems as the body wears out in old age.

There is growing belief that in both these psychoses the psychological changes attending old age are as much responsible as the organic changes, if not more so. There have been many recorded instances of recovery from these psychoses through the use of new physical and psychological treatment methods.

In psychosis with cerebral arteriosclerosis, the outstanding symptoms are confusion, agitation and excitement, restlessness, lessening of mental and physical capacity, incoherence, emotional instability with outbursts of laughing and weeping, impairment of memory, bewilderment, irritability, depression, anxiety, quarrelsomeness, aggressiveness, and outbursts of violence. The patient becomes neglectful of personal appearance. He frequently develops delusions of persecution.

In senile psychosis, there is a marked deterioration of the mental and emotional faculties. Intellective processes weaken, memory fails, ideas become meager, expression becomes bare and elementary. There is confusion about time and place. People are wrongly identified; living people are identified as people who have long been dead. Quarrelsomeness, suspiciousness, hoarding, stinginess, delusions of theft, of poisoning, and of being destitute are common. Interest in personal habits and control of personal sanitation are lost. The patient often wanders away and becomes lost, his judgment about safety and danger completely gone.

It is often difficult to distinguish between senile psychosis and psychosis with cerebral arteriosclerosis, since both types may be present at the same time.

Paranoia

Paranoid delusions of persecution are found in many psychotic conditions—in paranoid schizophrenia, in the psychoses of old age, in the depressive phase of manic-depressive psychosis, in involutional psychosis, and in depressive reaction.

In each of these illnesses, the paranoid condition is part of a larger disease complex in which a number of other symptoms are present. But there is a kind of mental illness—paranoia—in which the paranoid condition stands dominant, unaccompanied by other distinctive symptoms of mental disorder.

In paranoia, individual delusional ideas are replaced by a well-knit, well-integrated, comprehensive delusional system. The person with this illness imagines plots to hurt him, imprison him, or destroy him. The delusional system may also develop along lines of grandiosity in which the person imagines himself to possess great, even supernatural, importance and power.

CHAPTER FIVE

Alcoholism

Alcoholism is a chronic condition in which the individual is unable to refrain from the frequent consumption of alcohol in quantities sufficient to produce intoxication. The inability to refrain or the loss of control may be manifested in two ways. The individual may be unable to let a day go by without drinking heavily. Or he may have periods of sobriety between episodes of heavy and prolonged drinking, but once he begins to drink again he is unable to stop until he has drunk himself into unconsciousness. Both patterns are sometimes found in the same person, but usually only one is present.

Heavy and prolonged drinking does not in itself constitute alcoholism. There are millions of people who drink heavily and consistently out of a psychological need. They need alcohol as a crutch and cannot function well without it. Nevertheless there are times when they are able to reduce or even discontinue their alcohol intake without serious disturbance. In other words, they are not addicted.

According to prevailing theory, true alcoholism is an addiction. An alcohol addict cannot do without alcohol, for the same reason that a narcotics addict cannot do without narcotics. Continued use of alcohol, the theory holds, has produced a change in cell metabolism so that alcohol is needed for cell functioning (tissue need). When the system is deprived of alcohol, it expresses its "starvation" through withdrawal symptoms such as "the shakes," insomnia, depression, nausea, sweating, tachycardia, hallucinosis, and delirium tremens.

While heavy and prolonged drinking is a necessary prerequisite for the development of addictive alcoholism, only a small percentage of heavy drinkers ever become alcoholics. Some may go on drinking heavily for ten, twenty, or thirty years without becoming addicted. The relatively small number of heavy drinkers who do become addicted are believed to have a special physical susceptibility to alcohol addiction. There is no clue as yet as to the nature of this presumed physical susceptibility.

Alcoholism is not a distinct disease, but a disease condition found in association with many different psychiatric disorders including various psychoses, psychoneuroses, and personality disorders. It is a condition reached by many different paths—many different types of emotional disturbance operating in combination with different kinds of life stresses to which the person is particularly vulnerable. There is no single alcoholic personality especially prone to the development of alcoholism. There are many different kinds of disturbed personality that need and pursue the effects produced by alcohol. Ultimately, as a result of prolonged alcoholism, there emerges a characteristic alcoholic personality marked by

51

mental, emotional, and moral deterioration. This, however, is an end product and not a pre-existing condition.

Acute Alcoholism

The Withdrawal Syndrome

Prolonged alcoholism will produce a number of severe physical complications including heart ailments, gastritis, and liver damage, but the acute alcoholic toxic condition is primarily the withdrawal syndrome. Depending on the degree to which the withdrawal reaction has developed, the patient will be suffering from:

Psychomotor agitation and sensory confusion (first stage). The patient is subject to tics, spasms, sudden jerky movements, and other indications of uncontrollable nervous impulses. He stumbles frequently, is apt to miss his mouth when eating, is unable to locate the source of an itch or a pain, and may be unable to distinguish heat from cold (he may, for example, put on an overcoat on a sweltering hot day).

Hallucinosis (second stage). The individual hears voices that accuse him of immoral practices and threaten him with destruction and death. Otherwise the person remains in clear, accurate contact with his surroundings.

Delirium tremens (third, "full-blown" stage). Dramatic and film versions of delirium tremens have been quite accurate in their depictions. The victim suffers horrifying visual hallucinations in which animals of various sizes and shapes play an important part. His speech is incoherent. His body is in an almost constant state of tremor. He has little awareness of his surroundings and misidentifies people. He is in a wild nightmare, out of touch with reality.

Prior to the advent of the psychiatric drugs, such medications as paraldehyde, chloral hydrate, and the barbiturates were the only ones available for treatment of the acute toxic alcoholic condition. These have now been almost entirely replaced by the tranquilizers (see Chapter 8), which are, by almost unanimous agreement, highly effective, bringing about great improvement in a matter of hours. The psychiatric drug most frequently referred to as producing desired results is chlordiazepoxide (Librium). There is also considerable supportive evidence for the effective use of chlorpromazine (Thorazine), promazine (Sparine), triflupromazine (Vesprin), trifluoperazine (Stelazine), and thioridazine (Mellaril). The tranquilizer is generally given in combination with high vitamin doses, especially vitamin B.

Other Psychiatric Disorders
In addition to the withdrawal disturbances, other psychiatric disorders may also be present.

Alcoholic paranoia. The symptoms of alcoholic paranoia are suspiciousness, faultfinding, irritability, and jealousy with absurd delusions about the mate's infidelity. These suspicions may lead to hostile and even homicidal behavior.

Korsakoff's psychosis. One of the direct effects of prolonged, heavy intake of alcohol is vitamin B deficiency, resulting from sharply decreased consumption of food. The vitamin B deficiency acts destructively on the nervous system, causing impairment of the thought processes. The patient loses his sense of time and place, suffers loss of memory and makes up his past out of his head, so to speak, creating false memories of events that never happened. This condition, Korsakoff's syndrome, often follows delirium tremens but may develop independently. Discontinuance of alcohol and high vitamin B dosage will cause the disorder to abate.

Wernicke's syndrome. Another condition resulting from vitamin B deficiency and associated with chronic alcoholism is Wernicke's syndrome. The symptoms are disturbed functioning of vision, memory loss, confusion, wandering of the mind, stupor, and sometimes coma. Discontinuance of alcohol and dosing with vitamin B will cause this condition to clear up.

Alcoholic deterioration. After prolonged and sustained alcoholism, permanent injury to the nervous system brings about irreversible deteriorative changes both in personality and in mentality. Will, purpose, and interest are lost. Untruthfulness and unreliability, self-deception as to intent and achievement, and loss of feeling of responsibility become characteristic. There is general emotional deterioration, loss of ability to respond with warmth and affection, and difficulty in sex relations. The intellect also undergoes deterioration. Thoughts become cloudy, memory fails, reasoning ability collapses. At this stage there is little chance of reversal, as the mental and emotional deterioration are the product of irreparable damage to the nervous system.

Chronic Alcoholism

The treatment of the acute alcoholic state must be distinguished from the treatment of chronic alcoholism. The former attacks the immediate symptoms and seeks to restore normal body functioning. The latter attempts to reduce or break down the chronic addiction.

No thoroughly satisfactory treatment has yet been developed for the treatment of chronic alcoholism. While the tranquilizing drugs are effective in treating the acute symptoms, they do not appear to have much effect in controlling the addiction. The antidepressant drugs are useful in dealing with depression frequently found in the chronic condition.

Disulfiram (Antabuse), used as an abstinence-producing medication, is still regarded as one of the most effective devices for the control of chronic alcoholism. In the past, disulfiram was prescribed by itself. With the advent of special clinics and other treatment centers for the treatment of alcoholism, equal emphasis is now given to psychological therapy, including counseling, group activity, group psychotherapy, and participation in Alcoholics Anonymous (AA). Hospitals and outpatient clinics alike report the best result when all or most of these (including Antabuse) are used in combination. Great emphasis is given to continued, periodic follow-up contact with the patient at the hospital, clinic, rehabilitation center, or half-way house for months or even years. Few patients are able to maintain abstinence through their independent efforts and must continue to have the support of doctor, nurse, social worker, counselor, AA co-members, and others who have an interest in them and want to help them maintain their resolve. While AA is still regarded with skepticism by many nonpsychiatric physicians, most psychiatrists treating alcoholics welcome its participation in the treatment process. Many clinics and hospitals treating acute alcoholic patients have an AA unit operating within the treatment facility.

CHAPTER SIX

Psychosomatic Disorders

One does not need to be a psychiatrist to observe the many different physical processes that go along with the conscious experiencing of an emotion. Everyone has known the knotted-up feeling in the stomach, the dry mouth, the pounding heart, the flushed face, the trembling arms and voice, clenched fists, general muscular tension, and cold sweat that go with anger, fear, and apprehension.

Not only can such changes be recorded through instruments which measure blood pressure, pulse rate, respiration rate, muscular tension, and glandular secretion, but they can actually be seen with the eye. It is possible under certain laboratory conditions and with special instruments to observe the changes that occur in the organs of the body, particularly those of the digestive system. Under certain emotional conditions, the interior walls of the stomach can be seen to become engorged as blood rushes into the vast network of surface capillaries. In other emotional conditions, the surface of the stomach pales as blood rushes away from the stomach to other parts of the body.

Under some emotions, the movement of the intestinal tract is observed to speed up and in others to slow down. In some emotions, the secretion of digestive enzymes is increased; in others they are decreased.

Each different emotion—such as fear, anxiety, depression, grief, rage, guilt, or hate—is observed to produce a different combination of reactions in different parts of the digestive system, as well as in other internal parts of the body. Whenever any emotion is expressed, there is activity in the viscera, the "machinery of the emotions."

The stronger the emotion, the more powerful the visceral reaction. The longer the emotion is sustained, the greater is the duration of the visceral reaction. If the emotional state continues without letup, the internal visceral reaction also continues without letup. In people suffering from a neurosis, the repressed emotions of rage, fear, and hate continue to operate and to keep in a constant state of activity the internal organs through which they are normally expressed. When that happens, malfunctioning or injury to the organ or organs occurs, resulting in such illnesses as ulcers, asthma, colitis, chronic indigestion, hypertension, diabetes, and heart trouble.

These are not imaginary illnesses. These are real physical illnesses, physical illnesses that have been known to medicine for hundreds of years. What is new about them is that they are now known to be often caused by emotional (psychological) conditions. When they are, they are called psychophysiological illnesses or psychosomatic illnesses. (*Psyche* is the Greek word for "mind," *soma* for "body.")

High Blood Pressure

When a person is attacked or threatened with attack—whether physically or verbally—the body prepares itself automatically for counterattack. Among the many bodily changes which occur in this mobilization for action are a constriction of the blood vessels and a resultant increase in the blood pressure. Simultaneously the person experiences the emotion of anger. Ordinarily, the anger is vented through counterattack or channeled into some safe substitute emotion like contempt or philosophical resignation, and the body returns to a normal state. But with people who have repressed their emotions the demobilization does not occur and the blood vessels remain in a state of constriction. This is believed to be the explanation for many cases of high blood pressure (vascular hypertension).

It is not at all uncommon for a case of high blood pressure which had lasted for years to disappear suddenly as the psychological conditions change. This is often brought about by a removal from the environment of a person or situation that has been bringing out a neurotic anger response set up in early childhood. Relief comes, also, for reasons not yet known, when the repressed rage finds expression in some psychological symptom such as depression. One theory is that depression occurs when a person turns his anger and rage inward on himself.

The personality of many hypertensive patients is one of outward calm and friendliness, which masks a repressed hostility and aggressiveness. Another personality type which is often found in hypertensive people is the compulsive perfectionist. Compulsiveness and perfectionism are believed to be ways in which the psyche represses and controls hostile, aggressive impulses. Repressed out of consciousness, the anger and hostility persist through the bodily disturbance—hypertension.

Digestive Disorders

Peptic ulcer. It has been known for a long time that stomach ulcers have a psychological cause; along with this knowledge, there has developed a popular notion that ulcers are an illness common to pushers, drivers, ambitious go-getters—and that it is brought about by the intense pressures and extreme responsibility to which such people subject themselves. This characterization of the ulcer-prone patient is incorrect. The ulcer patient is likely to be just the opposite kind of person—calm, sweet, passive, or lazy and irresponsible.

The most commonly accepted theory about the cause of ulcers is that they are related to repressed feelings of dependency. These feelings may be as common in the aggressive, responsible, individualistic go-getter as in the passive, nonaggressive, unadventurous stay-at-home. Dependency, as used in psychological terminology, does not mean helplessness and the inability to do things for oneself. It means unusual and excessive attachment to another person—one who is a source of love and emotional protection. Such a person may be the mother or a person who in later life takes the place of the mother as a source of emotional sustenance.

When the dependency attachment is threatened, there is an anxiety reaction in which certain physiological processes take place in many parts of the body, including the stomach. One of these is the increased secretion of digestive juices. Another is the spastic closure of the pylorus (the duct between the stomach and the intestines). Together, these physical changes tend—so the theory goes—to keep the acid juices in the stomach eating away at the stomach walls, which are also

59

excessively sensitized by the engorgement of the surface blood vessels.

The dependency tie may be threatened in many different ways—by actual or threatened rejection by the loved one, by loss of or separation from the loved one, or by the punitive attitude of the loved one, who in such cases might be a domineering mother, wife, or husband. Such situations arouse the resentment and anger of the dependent person, and the state of chronic anger acts further to perpetuate the physical disturbance leading to stomach ulcers.

Ulcerative colitis. Ulcers of the colon accompanied by disturbed bowel functioning is another illness of the digestive system considered by many to have emotional causes. This tends to be more an acute than a chronic condition, with the attacks occurring customarily several weeks after some disturbing event, in which the person's feeling of emotional security is threatened. Such situations include bereavement through death, separation, or rejection, failure in school work or on the job or in some important interpersonal relationship.

Case histories of patients with ulcerative colitis often show conflict with a domineering, antagonistic, and rejecting mother. This kind of relationship develops a predisposition to expect humiliation and rejection. When in later life such people experience a situation in which rejection or humiliation is encountered, they react to it as they did in childhood—with resentment and rage which they repress following a pattern established in childhood. The repressed rage finds expression through physiological changes in the colon normally accompanying rage. Because of the intensity and continuity of the repressed emotion, the physiological processes are maintained at a high and continuous level, resulting in illness of the colon.

60

Transitory disorders. There is a large variety of transitory disturbances of the digestive system resulting from the emotional disturbances of neurosis and psychosis. These include heartburn, indigestion, stomach cramps, diarrhea, constipation, "gas," nausea, loss of appetite, and vomiting. While any one of these symptoms may develop into a chronic illness accompanying a specific psychological condition, they occur most often in connection with acute states of anxiety, depression, guilt, anger, or fear. They tend to be relieved as the situation is altered and the emotional disturbance relieved.

Obesity

Obesity has long been thought to be a constitutional condition resulting from glandular disturbances; it is now believed in a great many cases to have a psychological cause.

Obesity generally begins in childhood, and it is most often found in a nonassertive child from whom the parents get very little direct enjoyment and whom they use to compensate for their own frustrations and disappointments (including disappointment in their other children).

In such cases, the mother attaches herself to this child, becomes very anxious about his well-being and health, and stuffs him with food. Into this presumed concern about the child's well-being is fed the mother's own anxiety about herself. The more the child eats, the greater is the relief from her own anxiety; the greater is her own reassurance, misconceived, of course, that this child will become big and strong and fulfill for the mother all her own frustrated desire for comfort, love, and happiness.

After a while, the intake of food becomes not only physiologically habitual but emotionally habitual as well. There is satisfaction derived from it—not only in the enjoyment of the food but in the enjoyment of being the center of the mother's attention. Soon it also provides the child with the illusion of being big and powerful. The tolerant attention given to obese people provides them with an additional source of satisfaction, the feeling that they are special. And then, because obesity is a hindrance in love, work, and social relationships, the condition becomes an excuse and rationalization for failure.

Attempts to bring about weight reduction through dieting encounter numerous resistances and cannot be successful, without further emotional complications, unless the individual finds motivation strong enough to compensate for what he gives up when he decreases his intake of food.

Self-Starvation (*Anorexia nervosa*)

Long before psychiatry came into being, people knew about the disturbing loss of appetite in times of great emotional upset, especially during episodes causing anxiety, fear, worry, or depression. In such instances, normal bodily functioning is disturbed as the body goes through preparations for defensive or aggressive action. As the situation passes, normal functioning is restored and with it, appetite.

There are some conditions, however, in which there is a persistent and extreme lack of appetite unassociated with any physical disorder to account for it. One such illness has been identified as *anorexia nervosa*, a form of self-starvation.

This condition occurs mostly in young single women. Such patients are usually intellectually superior and manifest extremely self-centered personality traits. They are generally neurotic and of the compulsive-obsessive type. The loss of appetite is often accompanied by other physical disorders such as constipation and amenorrhea (absence of menstrual periods).

Many of these cases show conflict between mother and daughter, and frequently there is jealousy of a sister or brother. The "self-starvation" of these patients has the effect of controlling the other members of the family, frightening them, and making them sympathetic. In addition, these patients are given to provocative behavior, invoking punishment. This, it is theorized, "helps" them by relieving suppressed feelings of guilt which are believed to underlie the physical symptoms.

Rheumatoid Arthritis

Rheumatoid arthritis is characterized by painful inflammation of the joints and persisting stiffness, swelling, and deformity. This disease frequently occurs during a period of great emotional stress related to such traumatic or tragic events as the death of a parent or the separation from or rejection by a loved one.

The rheumatoid patient is one whom others would least suspect of having emotional problems. He is cheerful, outgoing, pleasant. He seldom expresses his feelings and appears to derive great pleasure out of service to others. He is generally quite active in physical or intellectual pursuits and prefers outdoor and competitive sports.

The psychological component of this illness appears to consist of repressed feelings of hostility, rebellion, anger, and guilt. These feelings, it is believed, arise out of conflict between the patient—as a child—and his parents. The characteristic family pattern in these cases consists of a domineering, controlling mother and a quiet, compliant father. The child is subdued by the mother and develops hostile, antagonistic feelings toward her. This produces fear of retaliation as well as guilt, both of which are repressed. In order to keep these feelings under control, the theory holds, the person develops strong, confident, outgoing feelings and activities, which also serve to control and dominate the environment. This produces the picture of the outgoing, capable, cooperative, generous person.

Migraine Headache

Headache has long been known to be associated with tension and anxiety. Sometimes the emotional cause of the headache is easily identifiable in the environment in the form of financial problems, strain and overwork, quarrels with family members and other such difficulties. Problem situations are actually referred to as "headaches." But headaches may also come from unconscious causes, from anxiety or other emotions which have been repressed but which continue to activate physical changes in the body. The physical change involved in a headache is the expansion of veins and arteries in the brain and the increased flow of blood through them.

The type of headache most likely to be caused by intensely disturbing and deeply repressed emotions is the migraine headache. This is a severe, blindingly painful headache, usually affecting one side of the head, and often accompanied by nausea, vomiting, constipation or diarrhea, urinary frequency, and a peculiar "aura"—a visual disturbance in which one part of the field of vision is clouded, focusing is impaired, and zigzag flashes of light are seen inside the eye. There is extreme, excruciating sensitivity to loud sounds and bright lights.

Migraine occurs most frequently in people between 15 and 35; in women, it often comes with the onset of menstruation. It is sometimes called a familial headache, because it is often present in successive generations, especially in women. There is some indication of a true hereditary factor, but also of an imitative heredity, in which a daughter unconsciously imitates the mother.

Migraine is believed to result from unexpressed anger. Its relationship to menstruation seems to indicate an angry and unrecognized rejection of the womanly role and its responsibilities. Its occurrence, generally in situations in which the person is called upon to assume adult responsibilities and to stand alone, appears to be related to an unusually strong attachment to the mother and an unwillingness to sever it. At the same time there is a repression of a great anger against the mother because of her part in perpetuating this dependency tie.

Asthma

While asthma may occur at any age, its first onset is most commonly experienced in childhood. Even when it occurs for the first time in adult life, it is related psychologically to a condition developed in childhood. People who suffer from asthma are generally overanxious and emotionally insecure. Their mothers, too, are overanxious, especially about the child. Sometimes this overanxiety stems from the fact that the child has been desperately wanted. Other times it stems from the very opposite feeling—a strong dislike and rejection of an unwanted child, feelings which are then covered up by an oversolicitousness.

In either case, the child is fussed over and overprotected to such an extreme degree as to give him a feeling of great helplessness, and a persevering anxiety about losing the protective care of the mother.

Attacks of asthma occur in situations in which the child fears he might lose his mother's love and protection, either through psychological rejection or through actual separation as in sickness or death.

While the psychological component in the cause of most cases of asthma is undisputed, there is recognition of predisposing allergic sensitivity. This sensitivity is acted upon by chemicals in the blood, causing the choking spasms of the lungs. While psychiatrists of the orthodox psychoanalytic school believe asthma to be symbolically a cry for help (an expressive plea for protection) or a cry of protest (in anger against the rejector), other schools of psychiatry hold that chemical substances released in the blood through fear of separation from the mother, or in protest against her overprotective hold, act on the allergic sensitivity of the respiratory system to cause the asthmatic spasm.

Diabetes

Since there is nothing as "physical" as the increased level of sugar in the blood and urine, and the reduction of these sugar levels through injection of insulin, one might tend to question the label "psychosomatic" applied to diabetes. Yet some psychiatrists consider it among the more striking examples of the influences of emotional disturbances on somatic functioning.

Attacks of diabetes often follow periods of severe emotional distress after long periods of grinding work or severe disturbances in the normal pattern of family life. While no distinct personality pattern has been identified in relation to diabetes, there is frequently evident a frustration because of unmet demands for love. Many cases indicate that the traumatic emotional reaction is caused by threat of rejection by, or deprivation of, a loved one, reactivating a threat experienced in childhood.

Open and active hostility and depression are found frequently in diabetic patients, especially in the periods when there is cause for feeling uncared for or rejected. Both psychological conditions (hostility and depression) as well as the physiological condition (diabetes) are relieved when the patient feels accepted and cared for.

The physical basis for diabetes is believed to be a predisposition to faulty sugar metabolism, which is then acted upon in some way by the psychological condition. Increase in sugar level is a normal bodily response in threatening situations (one of the many changes which prepare the body to flee or fight). Why it goes out of control in the stress situations to which diabetics appear particularly sensitive is not known.

CHAPTER SEVEN

Personality Disorders

In the discussion of the development of neurotic responses (Chapter 2), it was mentioned that a child develops a problem personality trait as a way of dealing with the unbearable conflict between his desire for gratification of his sensual needs and his need to keep his mother's love.

There are people who develop distorted personality characteristics not as a secondary neurotic response, but as a primary disorder, unaccompanied by the tension, anxiety, and mental and physical symptoms which are generally manifested by the neurotic person. Some theories hold that personality disorders result from an inborn defect. Others attribute the defective personality to the absence of one or both parents in the child's infancy, or their failure or inability to give the child the necessary freedom, love, guidance, strength, discipline, and direction for the shaping and development of a healthy personality. Some theories combine the two—the hereditary and parental influences.

The following are the most common personality disorders.

Inadequate Personality

Good-natured, easygoing, ineffective people who have little interest in work or study, a poor sense of responsibility, and an inability to grow through social or formal education are said to have an inadequate personality. In ordinary language they are referred to as drifters, floaters, or ne'er-do-wells.

Explosive Personality

This personality disorder is characterized by highly exaggerated, explosive responses to minor frustrations, disappointments, or rejections. Such behavior is clearly comparable to infantile rage except that in an adult the explosion may go so far as physical assault or suicide.

The explosive personality is characterized by such antagonistic behavior as being caustically critical and belittling of others; being contrary, dictatorial, and argumentative; and attempting to intimidate others by assaultive behavior and to put them on the defensive.

A person with this type of personality will tend to form superficial relationships with others, viewing them not as equals, but as stepping stones to the fulfillment of his own needs. Yet, in spite of all this, such a person might, under normal, unstressful circumstances, present the picture of a genial, well-adjusted individual.

Passive-Aggressive Personality

The passive-aggressive personality has three main characteristics: intense, unmanageable feelings of anger and hostility; fear that expression of these aggressive feelings will provoke retaliation; retreat into a passive role to circumvent expressing aggression; hence the designation passive-aggressive. There are two types. One becomes passive by assuming a docile, dependent, helpless demeanor. The other does so by passive resistance—that is, through stubbornness, sullenness, obstructiveness, and inefficiency.

Obsessive-Compulsive Personality

A person with an obsessive-compulsive personality is overinhibited, rigid, formal, perfectionistic. He has an exaggerated sense of duty and obedience. He is stubborn in his convictions and extremely self-centered. He has an excessive need to dominate the situation in which he works or lives so that he can control every detail and every element of his surroundings. If things are not done exactly the way he wants them done, he experiences great anxiety and anger. He finds it difficult to work under supervision because this means doing things another person's way, which may be different from his own. On the other hand, when he is in a supervisory position, he is unable to yield responsibility to others for fear they will not perform according to his perfectionist standards.

A person with an obsessive-compulsive personality is likely to postpone or avoid marriage because of his or her highly perfectionist expectations.

Exploration of the background of the obsessive-compulsive personality will often reveal the overly "good" child, obedi-

70

ent, compliant, conscientious to a fault, and given to occasional explosions of anger brought on by a simmering resentment against this docile role.

Antisocial Personality

A person with an antisocial personality is also known as a psychopath or sociopath. People with this personality disorder are lacking in conscience, feelings of humanity, honesty, or responsibility. They know the difference between right and wrong but do not care. They are concerned only with getting gratification and enjoyment when they want it, no matter how fraudulent, destructive, hurtful, or violent they have to be to get it. They are extremely cruel, unstable, unreliable, insincere, and easily provoked to violence. They are unable to form meaningful relationships with others, demanding much and giving little. They feel no concern that others dislike or fear them. They are satisfied with themselves.

Many of the people with antisocial personality disorders are quite intelligent and pleasant in their manner and find it easy to impress and deceive others. Examples are the confidence man, the check forger, the bigamist or polygamist. Others are quite different in their attitude and demeanor—the 'punks," hoodlums, and professional killers.

Paranoid Personality

The person with a paranoid personality is characterized by suspiciousness, oversensitivity, jealousy, resentment, and hosility. He is extremely sensitive to criticism and takes minor corrections as devastating attacks. He has a very low estimate of himself and thinks that others think poorly of him, too;

that they dislike him and shun him, and that they pick on him and ridicule him.

This provokes in him a drive to compensate for his imagined inadequacies and to set goals far beyond his capabilities. Failure to achieve these goals deepens his sense of personal failure and intensifies his resentment against the world. He goes about with a chip on his shoulder and is highly critical of others, whom he must cut down to ease the injury to his own self-esteem.

He tends to blame his failure on others. In addition, he is prone to attribute to others hostile feelings which are within himself but which he cannot acknowledge (this process is called projection).

His hostile, defensive, critical behavior tends to antagonize others and thus to deepen his own sense of isolation. Soon he sees his misfortune as not accidentally but deliberately caused. It is no longer a matter of not getting the breaks but a matter of being victimized. People not only dislike him but go out of their way to insult him, hurt him, deprive him, keep him down. He no longer feels just hurt; he feels wronged, even persecuted. This sense of persecution permeates his whole thinking process and he sees enemies and plots everywhere.

When the condition reaches this stage of intensity, irrationality, and unrealistic evaluation, it changes from paranoid personality to psychotic paranoia. (A paranoid personality does not necessarily develop into paranoia. A person may remain a paranoid personality all his life without becoming psychotic.)

Schizoid Personality

In many respects the schizoid personality resembles the early stages of psychotic schizophrenia but is not considered psychotic because there is no disintegration of the personality as there is in schizophrenia.

The schizoid personality is characterized by shut-in-ness and emotional detachment from other people and from things and events outside himself. While the schizoid personality carries on the fundamental functions of life, he does so with minimum investment of true interest in his surroundings and a minimum relatedness to the people and events around him. His deepest involvement and most intense feelings are experienced internally in daydreams, imaginings, and fantasy.

The schizoid is apt to feel lonely, misunderstood, isolated. He is always feeling "wounded." He feels no one wants him or thinks well of him, but his suspicious nature will cause him to resist attempts of others to become friendly and draw him out. As a child he stays away from other children and their games, preferring to be by himself. He is likely to spend a great deal of time reading, either comics or good literature, depending on his intelligence and background. Child or man, few people know what he is thinking because he confides in nobody.

The schizoid person of high intelligence and great sensitivity may be very creative and productive in artistic and intellectual endeavors. He will appear to be a sensitive, frail, esthetic, gentle person, but unfriendly and remote. The less intelligent and less sensitive schizoid person will appear dull, disagreeable, sullen, mistrustful, headstrong, and uncooperative. Occasionally, a mixture of these qualities is found in the same person.

Cyclothymic Personality

The person with a cyclothymic personality tends to swing from moods of excitement, enthusiasm, optimism, and joyful activity to moods of dejection, gloominess, pessimism, and futility. He is generally regarded as an interesting person and attracts many friends, but his unpredictability makes him difficult to get along with. His moods may range from elation to depression, but are seldom extreme in either direction.

Hysterical Personality

This disorder, which is more prevalent in women than in men, is characterized by dramatic, histrionic, affected, attention-getting behavior embellished by lies and elaborate fantasies. People with this personality disorder have a tendency to read into the motives of others a great deal more than is really there. A simple act of polite friendship may be seen as romantic infatuation, or an ordinary minor criticism might be interpreted as an act of envious hostility.

They often employ a seductive manner, which covers fear and uncertainty about sex, even frigidity. They appear to have an insatiable need for love and affection together with an inability to respond to it when offered.

It is difficult for the hysterical personality to verbalize feelings or to be precise about emotions. People with this disorder are characteristically vague and confused. Words tumble out but give no indication of what is really being felt. Extravagant gestures are used in a vain effort to provide the meaning which speech is unable to convey.

CHAPTER EIGHT

Treatment
of Mental Illness

Treatment of mental illness can deal with the thoughts and
emotions themselves, or it can deal with the machinery of the
mind and emotions—the brain, nervous system, glands,
circulatory system, and so on. The first method is called
psychotherapy; the second is called physical therapy or
somatotherapy.

Psychotherapy

There are many different kinds of psychotherapy. In all of
them, the basic method involves a verbal and emotional
interchange between the patient and the therapist, in the
course of which there is an alteration of the patient's thoughts
and feelings and a lessening or complete elimination of the
mental and physical symptoms.

Psychoanalysis

In psychoanalysis, the patient's troublesome feelings and emotions are probed and analyzed in an attempt to trace them back to their origins, to find out what caused them to develop as they did, to understand them in the light of past experiences. This type of treatment has a double purpose. When hidden emotions and conflicts are unearthed, they no longer require indirect expression and the symptoms disappear. Secondly, the understanding (insight) gained by the patient in the process helps him to eliminate useless, harmful, destructive ways of feeling and behaving and to develop new, effective, appropriate, and healthy ways.

Because repressed thoughts and emotions are not available to conscious recall, it is necessary to use methods which will get around the repressing mechanism that operates constantly to keep them from coming into consciousness.

One such method is free association, in which the patient speaks out everything that comes to mind, even if it sounds like utter nonsense. As conscious control relaxes, the patient blurts out thoughts and feelings that had been kept buried in the unconscious mind.

Another method is dream analysis. Although dreams may appear to be jumbled, nonsensical, and meaningless, they are full of hidden meaning which gives important clues to the repressed thoughts and emotions. People in dreams are disguised versions of the key people in the patient's life—mother, father, sisters and brothers, the psychoanalyst, the patient himself. The things which the "characters" in the dream say and do are disguised expressions of the patient's own feelings, generally feelings which he cannot admit to himself. With the help of the analyst, the patient tries to penetrate the disguises and to recognize what, underneath, he really feels and thinks.

As the digging and probing touches on sensitive areas and threatens to bring to the surface very painful feelings, the repressing force springs into action to thwart the exposure, causing the patient to block. His mind goes blank and he is unable to think of anything to say. This process is known as resistance. Resistance also takes other forms—forgetting psychoanalytic appointments or coming late for them; inability to bring to mind other than routine, unimportant subjects for psychoanalytic discussion; discontent with the psychoanalyst or with psychoanalysis as a whole. The psychoanalyst helps the patient to recognize he is evading the real issues and works with him in overcoming the resistance.

As the psychoanalytic process continues, the patient reacts to the analyst as though he were the mother or father of his infancy, venting on the analyst the strong feelings which he had had for these key people in his life. This is called transference, a crucial phase in the psychoanalytic process. Without transference, psychoanalysis cannot succeed. As the transference proceeds, the patient reenacts with the psychoanalyst (the "parent") the original conflict of childhood. Only now, in the present, he finds that the "parent" does not punish, does not reject, does not stifle, does not suppress as did the true parent.

The emotions forbidden in childhood—hate, hostility, dependency, greed, love—can now be felt without the need for repression. Once accepted and expressed, they lose their power to generate the symptoms of mental illness, and the symptoms disappear.

The distorted, fear-ridden, guilt-ridden attitudes developed in the course of the original conflict (in response to parental rejection and punishment) can now be discarded and replaced by healthy attitudes formed in a new relationship with a new "parent"—the unpunishing, non-rejecting psychiatrist. As these attitudes toward the "parent" change, so do they change toward other people—the mate, children, neighbors, employers, and so forth.

In this process, the individual truly gives up the persistent, exaggerated cravings of infancy—for protection, for dependency, for mastery, for sensual gratification. These cravings no longer have any meaning or force and are now relinquished. Instead, the individual expresses himself and relates to other people in terms of mature, adult desires and needs.

The neurotic mechanism of childhood is broken up and the patient is freed to live in the present—to live a life of conscious choice, determining for himself what his relationship will be to the world and to other people, rather than having these relationships determined for him by the fears, hates, guilts, and greeds of childhood.

Psychoanalytically Oriented Psychotherapy

Psychotherapy may use psychoanalytical methods without the intensity or depth of true psychoanalysis. The goals of such psychoanalytically oriented psychotherapy are to strengthen and perhaps reshape the personality, but not necessarily to rebuild it as in psychoanalysis. Psychoanalytically oriented psychotherapy does not attempt to bring about reenactment of the conflicts and emotional struggles of childhood, nor does it attempt to undo the fundamental neurotic pattern formed in the course of these struggles.

It does attempt to bring about the expression of repressed emotions through free association and dream analysis, but it is more concerned with the emotions being repressed in connection with the immediate situation than those repressed in childhood.

The patient is helped to gain understanding of and insight into some of the causes of his neurotic symptoms, without going any further back than necessary. He is helped to see that his present way of relating to other people and the handling of his conflicts with these people are exaggerated, distorted, and inappropriate. Then he is helped to shape appropriate, effective ways. With the acceptance and expression of repressed emotions, the symptoms are reduced in intensity, and with the reshaping of attitudes, difficulties in handling life's problems are reduced.

All this is done as an overlay on the neurotic pattern, which continues to persist and operate but which can now be modified by a new, additional self-control and by the release and diversion of some of the emotional energy which had previously gone into the operation of the neurotic pattern.

Supportive Therapy

There is a type of psychoanalytically oriented psychotherapy which does not have as its goal the expression of repressed emotions or the achievement of insight into the underlying causes of the neurotic symptoms. It is called supportive therapy and is used mainly on a short-term basis to help the patient through an emotional crisis, such as divorce, the death of a relative, or failure in profession or business. It has been successfully used in combatting suicidal fears and the acute onset of anxiety, phobia, or depression.

Supportive therapy strives to relieve the patient of his symptoms by giving him reassurance, confidence, and emotional support. The therapist acts in the role of protective parent, permitting the patient to lean on him to the fullest extent for a sense of safety and human warmth. The patient is relieved, for the duration of supportive therapy, of the necessity to make important decisions while the therapist gives him advice and even assistance in handling his practical problems. Supportive therapy provides a period of dependence during which the patient obtains relief from the intensely disturbing emotions which beset him—anxiety, guilt, shame, loneliness—which he cannot handle by himself.

If tranquilizers or antidepressant drugs are needed, they are prescribed. In a case of extreme disturbance, hospitalization may be required.

Supportive therapy may also be used on a long-term basis with patients who are almost continually on the edge of emotional crisis, even in the absence of any extreme precipitating incident, and who need continuous support.

There are some patients whose ego is so fragile that they cannot tolerate the unearthing and disclosure of repressed emotions, and who therefore cannot be treated with psychoanalysis or psychoanalytically oriented therapy. Supportive therapy serves, for these patients, to keep the unacceptable emotions safely repressed, and provides them supportive strength from the outside to maintain internal emotional equilibrium.

Group Therapy

The types of psychotherapy thus far discussed are based on the interaction between the patient and one other person, the therapist. In group therapy the patient interacts not only with the therapist but with a number of other patients, who make up the group.

The therapist sits with anywhere between five and twenty patients. Different situations and different types of patients determine whether the group is to be small or large.

In this setting, the patient brings into play a larger range and variety of emotions than he would with the individual therapist. In individual therapy, he might tell the therapist how he feels about other people. In group therapy he acts out his feelings about other people—the other people in the group. A degree of transference occurs not only toward the therapist but also toward the other patients in the group. The therapist remains the key figure for each patient, but other key figures emerge, too—patients who are seen as resembling individuals who have played key roles in the patient's early life.

The patients talk to each other and to the therapist. Fears are expressed, strong emotions are voiced, hostilities spill out, aggressive or passive or negativistic roles are assumed. Slowly, changes take place. New facets of the personality of each of the patients come out—less defensive, less fearful, more protective of each other, more concerned about the therapist, about the group. More humor and greater relaxation appear as members of the group learn to turn outward.

With extremely sick patients, delusions fade, hallucinations disappear, agitated behavior quiets down, depression yields to an interest and liveliness. With not-so-sick patients, the anxieties and depressive states are lessened, compulsive acts become less fixed, phobias lose their hold.

Group therapy is not regarded as either inferior or superior to individual therapy but as another type of therapy. It may be used instead of individual psychotherapy because it is more opportune to do so or because a particular condition might be considered to be more susceptible to group therapy than to individual therapy. The two are frequently used in conjunction. In private sessions the therapist explores with the individual, in greater depth and on a much more intimate individual basis, personality facets and problems which come into evidence in group sessions.

Group therapy sometimes makes use of a special technique called *psychodrama*. The patients are asked to dramatize, as though they were on stage, a scene concerned with a key emotional problem. In the process of dramatization, the patient is likely to be freed of his self-consciousness and conscious control and to tap hidden emotions and conflicts which might not have come out in the direct interchange of individual psychotherapy or group therapy.

Family Therapy

Family therapy is a relatively new form of treatment, having come into fairly common use only during the 1960s. It is based on the theory that a psychiatrically sick individual is evidence of a psychiatrically sick family; that it is not alone the "presenting person" (the patient who comes for treatment) who is in need of treatment, but rather the entire family. It is not the purpose of family therapy to "get to the family" in order to help the one family member who has come for help, but rather to treat a condition which pervades the entire family. In that way, not just the one family member is helped, but also all the others, who, it is generally found, are also suffering from various types and degrees of emotional, social, and psychosomatic disorders.

It will be many years before families become aware of themselves as a psychiatrically sick group and come for help together; however, family therapy does not necessarily have to be initiated in that way and seldom is. Customarily, it is begun as an adjunct to the psychiatric treatment of one family member. Whether or not the whole family is called in, depends on the orientation of the person or persons giving treatment, as well as on the patient and the family themselves. A practitioner or facility that does not give family therapy may refer a patient to a practitioner or facility that does.

Family therapy makes use of a number of different approaches. Where possible, the entire family is seen together in a group. In addition, family members may be seen in individual psychotherapy, and in groups of two or three.

Family psychotherapy also makes use of vector therapy,

82

which consists mainly of manipulating the practical situation so as to relieve some acute stress. If, for example, the family conflict is aggravated by the presence of a psychotic grandmother, efforts will be made to remove her from the scene; if a child has difficulty in nursing because the mother is antagonistic or withdrawn, other feeding arrangements are made.

Family therapy is used quite frequently in the treatment of patients with marital problems, the assumption being that marital discord is produced by individual psychiatric problems of both partners and by the sick interaction of all the family members. The couple coming for marital therapy will be seen together as well as separately. They may also be involved in group therapy with other couples. If it is practical to do so, the children may be brought in, as well as the parents of one or both mates. It is frequently found that the "lateral" marital discord—the discord between husband and wife—is the projection of a "vertical" discord—one between the man or wife and his or her own parents, or one or more of their children. When the vertical discords are worked out, the lateral discord will often disappear.

Behavior Therapy

Behavior therapy ignores the repressed unconscious emotions and regards the symptom simply as a "bad habit" which needs to be unlearned.

Behavior therapy is based on the proposition that behavior is maintained by its consequences. Pleasure-giving, rewarding consequences reinforce the behavior and increase the probability of its being repeated. Neutral or negative consequences decrease the probability of repetition and bring about the extinction of the behavior.

A child was brought to a mental health center because of very severe stomach pains which kept him disabled and prevented him from going to school. Medical examination failed to reveal an organic cause, yet the pain was real, and there was evidence of spasms in the large intestine.

A number of approaches were possible. Medication might be given to relax the intestinal muscles. Or psychoanalytically oriented psychotherapy might be given to probe the conflict between mother and child and to bring about expression of the child's repressed fear of separation from the mother, which was manifesting itself in spasms of the intestines.

Behavior therapy offered a third alternative: Do not comfort the child when he complains about the pain. The mother was advised to listen to the child and to express concern but to withhold any patting, cuddling, or sympathetic baby talk. At first, this sharp alteration in the mother's response produced an intensification of the symptoms, lasting for several days. Then the symptoms began to abate and within a few days were gone.

Another case illustrates the extinction of a phobic reaction by the process of desensitization. In essence, desensitization is achieved by presenting the threatening, phobia-provoking situation over and over again, first in very weak doses and then in increasingly powerful doses until it no longer evokes the phobic reaction. This is carried on simultaneously with the induction of an emotional state which runs counter to fear, such as relaxation or pleasure.

A woman of 32 came to a clinic for treatment because she was unable to go out of her house unless she was in the company of her husband or another member of her family. If she attempted to go out alone, she would experience extreme anxiety bordering on panic. This had been going on for more than ten years. The patient had a history of a heart disorder, which helped her to maintain a posture of helplessness and reinforce the phobic condition which kept her dependent on her husband, and her husband tied to her.

At first, the patient was trained in deep muscle relaxation, a simple process, learned in a few sessions, which enabled her to put one set of muscles after another—neck, eyes, diaphragm, arms, and so forth—into a state of complete relaxation.

Then the therapist constructed a hierarchy of fear-eliciting stimuli related to the condition, starting with one that was almost benign and ascending to one that was certain to elicit extreme fear. The most benign in this case was the word "alone." First the patient was asked to put herself in a state of relaxation. Then she was asked to think of the word "alone." If this produced anxiety, she was instructed to stop thinking about it and to substitute for it a pleasant image of a scene at the beach. Then the "alone" stimulus was tried again. When it no longer produced anxiety, the therapist went to the next stimulus. He asked the patient to imagine her husband walking out of the room. This produced anxiety, and she was asked to stop imagining it and to think instead of a beach scene. Then it was tried again, and so on up the scale until, toward the end of the series, she was able to imagine herself walking out to the store all by herself without experiencing anxiety. At each successful step, she was asked to sketch a word picture of what she was thinking, reinforcing the positive, anxiety-free experience. Also, as each new step was undertaken, the patient was asked to put herself in a state of relaxation.

When the imagining series was successfully completed, an actual life series was constructed. The husband, who, because of the wife's phobic condition, always accompanied her to the clinic, was first asked to leave the office and walk to another floor, then to walk out on the street, and eventually to stay away during the entire therapy session. Then the husband stopped coming to the clinic, and one of the children came with the patient instead; then a neighbor; then the patient came alone. After that a series of progressive situations was arranged, leading to the point where the patient went to the store by herself without experiencing any anxiety. Within a few months, the patient was completely free of her phobia.

Behavior therapy is not as yet used very widely, but it is being received favorably, even in facilities where traditional practice is firmly established. Follow-up research indicates a high degree of lasting success, especially with cases of phobia and compulsive-obsessive neurosis.

Physical Therapies

Psychiatric Drugs

The physical therapy most widely used for the mental illnesses is drug therapy. The psychiatric or psychotropic drugs fall into two main categories—tranquilizers and psychic energizers, or antidepressants.

The tranquilizers reduce anxiety, agitation, uncontrollable physical activity, destructiveness, hallucinations, and delusions.

The antidepressants, as their name implies, counteract depression, withdrawal, inactivity, stupor, delusions, and suicidal impulses.

Powerful tranquilizers such as chlorpromazine (Thorazine), trifluoperazine (Stelazine), thiothixene (Navane), thioridazine (Mellaril), haloperidol (Haldol), and perphenazine (Trilafon) are used mainly with psychotic patients suffering from schizophrenia, manic-depressive psychosis, senile psychosis, and acute alcoholism.

Antidepressants such as tranylcypromene (Parnate), isocarboxazid (Marplan), phenelzine (Nardil), doxepin hydrochloride (Sinequan), imipramine (Tofranil), amitriptyline (Elavil), and methylphenidate (Ritalin) are used in depressive illnesses such as involutional psychosis, reactive depression, the depressive phases of manic-depressive psychosis, alcoholism, senile psychosis, and acute neurotic depression.

While psychiatric drugs are most effective in combination with psychotherapy, practical conditions in the mental hospitals make it impossible to give either individual therapy or group therapy to more than a few patients. Nevertheless, research has demonstrated that even without psychotherapy, the psychiatric drugs can relieve many psychotic patients of some or all of their major symptoms. Many need to continue on drugs to avoid relapse. Others can do without them for long periods.

Psychiatric drugs are also effective with the neuroses. Tranquilizers such as diazepam (Valium), oxazepam (Serax), chlordiazepoxide (Librium), and meprobromate (Equanil and Milltown) are used to reduce neurotic anxiety and even mild depression. Many physicians prescribe them for physical conditions believed to result from neurotic tension, conditions such as insomnia, indigestion, fatigue, and headaches.

A psychotropic drug, which is neither a tranquilizer nor an antidepressant but which has demonstrated its effectiveness in controlling the manic phase of manic-depressive psychosis, is the simple chemical compound lithium carbonate. It is frequently used in sequence with one of the strong tranquilizers such as halperidol, chlorpromazine, or trifluoperazine. Some psychiatrists consider lithium an effective antidepressant and use it to control not only manic but also depressive episodes.

How the psychiatric drugs work is not known for certain, but research, so far, indicates the process to be as follows:

In the lower part of the brain, there is a control center for the emotions and the bodily systems involved in the emotions. This control center, the hypothalamus, is triggered by a group of glandular secretions, sometimes referred to as the trigger amines—adrenalin, noradrenalin, and seratonin—which go into action in situations where the person faces a threat. The emotions normally generated in such situations are fear, suspicion, and rage. In many mental illnesses, the sense of threat is highly exaggerated and is often based on imagination and fantasy. As a result, the trigger amines are constantly in action, stimulating excessive and abnormal emotions and abnormal bodily reactions.

The tranquilizers work by counteracting the trigger amines.

One type of tranquilizer, the phenothiazines (such as chlorpromazine) is believed to neutralize the noradrenalin. Another type of tranquilizer known as the Rauwolfia alkaloids (such as reserpine) is believed to force the trigger amines out of storage and to expose them to oxidation, thus burning them up before they can ever get into the bloodstream on the way to the hypothalamus.

The antidepressants also do their work by regulating the effectiveness of the trigger amines, but in the opposite direction: they work to *enhance* the action of these amines.

One group of antidepressants, the mono amine oxidase inhibitors, work by destroying the enzyme mono amine oxidase, the normal function of which is to oxidize (or burn up) excess secretions of amines in the bloodstream. In counteracting this enzyme, the antidepressants allow excess supplies of the trigger amines to accumulate and to act on the hypothalamus, thus stimulating additional bodily activity and emotional response. Another group of antidepressants are believed to act by making the cells of the hypothalamus more sensitive to the action of the trigger amines.

Shock Therapy

Until the psychiatric drugs came into use, the most widely used form of physical therapy was shock therapy—a form of therapy which renders the patient unconscious and through some still-unknown method results in a reduction or elimination of the symptoms. Shock treatment had been used to counteract depression, agitation, and withdrawal in schizophrenia, manic-depressive psychosis, involutional psychosis, and depressive reaction. Its most effective use has been in overcoming depression and other symptoms related to it. It continues to be used in many cases which do not yield to drug treatment.

The two most commonly used forms of shock treatment are insulin shock and electroshock.

In insulin shock, doses of insulin are injected, sharply reducing the level of sugar in the blood. The brain is thus deprived of its chief foodstuff, and the patient sinks into a coma. The use of insulin shock requires extensive medical and nursing supervision and hence is not widely used.

In electroshock, a light electric current is passed through the brain for a split second, inducing a convulsion. The patient loses consciousness. He has no awareness of what is happening and experiences no pain whatever. After a short time he regains consciousness, remaining in a somewhat confused state for several hours.

CHAPTER NINE

Who Treats Mental Illness and Where

Mental illness is treated by psychiatrists, psychoanalysts, psychologists, psychiatric social workers, and psychiatric nurses. Patients under treatment may live at home or in hospitals, depending on their condition and the type of treatment necessitated. The kinds of help available (including help for children) are described in this chapter; the next chapter will explain how such help may be obtained.

Professions

The Psychiatrist

The psychiatrist is a medical doctor who specializes in psychiatry, the branch of medicine concerned with the treatment of mental illness.

To become a psychiatrist, the doctor follows a prescribed course of training after graduation from medical school. This includes three years of service as a resident physician in an institution where mental illness is treated—a state mental hospital, the psychiatric section of a general hospital, a private mental hospital, or a mental health center. This is followed by two years of additional experience in this specialty. The final step is examination by the Board of Psychiatry and Neurology of the American Medical Association, the American Psychiatric Association, and the American Neurological Association. This board certifies the doctor as a psychiatrist. (A term commonly used is "board-certified.")

Residency training includes work with the physical therapies and with individual and group psychotherapy. The individual psychotherapy taught in residency does not include systematic training in psychoanalysis. The doctor who wants to practice psychoanalysis must go on for an additional course of training, generally for about two years in an institute for psychoanalysis.

The Psychoanalyst

The psychiatrist who has received the additional training and devotes his practice primarily to psychoanalysis is called a psychoanalyst. There are also nonmedical psychoanalysts. They are called lay analysts. The lay analyst is generally a psychologist who, after completing his training in clinical psychology, takes an additional course of study at a psychoanalytic institute.

The Clinical Psychologist

Psychology is not a branch of medicine. It is a branch of academic learning like sociology, mathematics, and physics.

It is concerned with every aspect of human behavior, normal and abnormal. The person who devotes most of his time to professional research or teaching in this field is called a psychologist. He will have either an MA, an MS, or a PhD degree. The PhD is awarded after three or four years of graduate study in psychology at a university. Psychologists who specialize in the study of abnormal behavior and the application of this knowledge in clinical settings are called clinical psychologists. In addition to their academic graduate work, clinical psychologists must also take an internship of one to two years at a psychiatric hospital or clinic. During this internship they receive training in administering psychological tests. Most internships also include training in individual and group psychotherapy. In their professional occupation in psychiatric hospitals, clinics, and mental health centers, clinical psychologists give psychological tests for diagnosis and prognosis. Many also give individual and group psychotherapy under the direction of a psychiatrist.

Some clinical psychologists go into private practice. Those who have had training in psychoanalytic institutes practice psychoanalysis as lay analysts. Those who practice non-analytic psychotherapy are called psychotherapists.

In many states, the state psychological association, a branch of the American Psychological Association, sets up standards and tests for certification of their members as accredited psychologists.

The Psychiatric Social Worker

The psychiatric social worker is a college graduate who has gone on to two years of postgraduate study in a school of social work, and has received the degree of MSW (Master of Social Work). If the social worker concentrates in the area of psychiatric case work, he or she is known as a psychiatric social worker. The student who concentrates on psychiatric social work will be assigned to field work in a mental hospital, a mental health clinic, a mental health center, or a family service agency that gives guidance, counseling, and therapy for clients with emotional problems. On graduation, the psychiatric social worker will go to work in one of these settings.

In the mental hospital or psychiatric service of a general hospital, the psychiatric social worker maintains contact between the patient and his family, serves as part of the treatment team, helps the family understand and adjust to the problems created by hospitalization of the relative, and supervises the social, economic, and vocational rehabilitation of the patient on his discharge from the hospital.

In the psychiatric clinic, the social worker sees the patient and his relatives when they first come for help and interprets the clinic to them. Once treatment has started, the social worker may give counseling or guidance to the relatives while the psychiatrist is treating the patient, or in some cases, administer psychotherapy under the direction of the psychiatrist.

When psychiatric social workers have gained sufficient experience in psychotherapy in a clinic or hospital, they may go into private practice as psychotherapists.

The National Association of Social Workers has a system of voluntary accreditation through which members who meet certain requirements for training and experience are accepted as members of the Academy of Certified Social Workers (ACSW).

The Psychiatric Nurse

Nurses receive their basic training either at the diploma level or the baccalaureate level. The diploma is received after three years of hospital training. The bachelor's degree in nursing (either BA or BS) is received after a four-year college program with a major in nursing.

Both these programs provide the nurse with a fundamental background in the nursing care of the psychiatric patient. In many state hospitals, community mental health centers, and the psychiatric services of general hospitals, the nurse involved in the care of mental patients is most likely to be a diploma nurse or a nurse with a bachelor's degree who has had on-the-job training in psychiatric nursing.

Specialized training in psychiatric nursing is received through a graduate program leading to a master's degree. The psychiatric nurse with this training is prepared to plan, implement, and evaluate the nursing care of psychiatric patients and to conduct inservice training programs in psychiatric nursing.

Hospital treatment of the mentally ill consists in large part of drug therapy and, to a lesser degree, shock therapy; the psychiatric nurse will be directly involved in these treatment processes.

In the past several years, psychiatric nurses have also been involved more and more as cotherapists in group psychotherapy, or as individual psychotherapists under the direction of the psychiatrist.

Where Mental Illness Is Treated

Private Practice

Private psychiatric practice varies greatly from one psychiatrist to another. Some psychiatrists will treat patients with all degrees of mental illness, including acute psychotic episodes, and give a wide range of treatment including supportive psychotherapy, intensive psychotherapy, and the psychiatric drugs. Some will also include electroshock where indicated for patients not requiring close and continuous medical supervision. Some psychiatrists will concentrate on patients with neuroses and restrict themselves to intensive psychotherapy in combination with drug therapy. Others concentrate exclusively on psychoanalytically oriented psychotherapy or on psychoanalysis.

Generally, the psychoanalyst will take only patients with varying degrees of neurosis, as this method is not considered effective with psychosis. During the 1930s and 1940s most psychoanalysts followed strictly the theory of the founder of psychoanalysis, Sigmund Freud; however, a number of schools of psychoanalysis have developed in the United States which have departed from or modified some of the fundamental concepts of Freud, giving much greater emphasis to the role of interpersonal relationships and social factors in the development of the neuroses. Also, many psychoanalysts today deal much more intensively with the patient's recent and present experiences and do not probe so deeply and minutely into the forgotten experiences of childhood.

Psychoanalysis today involves two or three sessions a week of 45 to 50 minutes each, and continues for two to three years. There is a growing tendency for psychoanalysts to combine individual therapy with group therapy and family therapy. Thus, a patient may be seen by his analyst in a private session, then in a session with his or her mate, or parents, or children, and then in a group session with a number of other patients.

The psychotherapist—the clinical psychologist or social worker—practices a less intensive form of psychoanalytically oriented psychotherapy and sees patients once or twice a week for periods ranging from a few months to two years.

The Psychiatric Clinic

The psychiatric clinic is an outpatient service for ambulatory patients in need of psychiatric care. The clinic originated several decades ago as a facility for children with emotional disturbances. Since then, many different patterns have emerged. Some clinics still take only emotionally disturbed children. Others take only children, but with varying degrees of illness, including childhood schizophrenia. Many clinics take patients of all ages and with all degrees of illness including psychosis, as well as patients in need of follow-up psychiatric treatment after discharge from the mental hospital.

Clinic treatment is built on the team approach, the team consisting of the psychiatrist, the psychiatric social worker, and the clinical psychologist. Generally the psychiatrist directs the clinic, directs other members of the staff in giving psychotherapy, and gives some treatment himself. The psychologist gives diagnostic and prognostic tests and conducts individual and group psychotherapy under the direction of the psychiatrist. The social worker does social case work with the patients and family, and conducts individual and group therapy under the direction of the psychiatrist. Clinics range in size from those having only the basic team of three to some having as many as twenty-five or more psychiatrists, psychologists, and social workers.

Psychiatric clinics are operated under a variety of auspices—some as outpatient services of general hospitals, some as adjuncts of the mental hospitals, some as part of a family service agency. Some operate in the community independent of any other service. In cases where the patient is a child, it is the practice of the clinic also to see the mother and the father, too, for separate psychotherapy. Many clinics have group therapy as well as family therapy.

The Family Service Agency

As originally conceived, the family service agency was designed to help people with life problems who were unable to help themselves—children in need of adoption, unwed mothers, families in financial straits, aged people in need of financial or medical aid or help in finding a home. This was social case work. With the advent of psychoanalysis, the nature of the work began to change. It is no longer the purpose of the agency merely to help people, but to help people mobilize their emotional resources so they can help themselves. When the situation indicates that the emotional problem is a primary cause rather than a contributing factor, the client is referred for psychiatric treatment. Recently many family agencies have begun to incorporate within their own structure treatment facilities in the form of psychiatric clinics. The psychotherapy is done by social workers under the direction of a psychiatrist.

The General Hospital

While psychiatry has been an established branch of medicine for many decades, medical treatment of the mentally ill under conditions and considerations similar to those applying to other illnesses has been deferred until quite recently. There were three major obstacles: One was the public prejudice about mental illness—shared also by much of the medical profession. No one wanted "crazy people" in the general hospital or in the community. Another was the concern that the bizarre and often unruly behavior of the psychotic patient would be disturbing to the functioning of the rest of the hospital. Third was the absence of a medical treatment for mental illness which could be easily administered in a regular hospital.

The psychiatric drugs quickly eliminated the second and third objections. They provided a form of treatment similar to treatment for other illnesses, and easily administered. They quieted the agitated patients and livened the depressed patients within a short time, eliminating behavior which might be disturbing to other patients, hospital staff, or residents of the community. In achieving this last change, they also helped to remove the first-mentioned obstacle—fear and prejudice.

As a result, the efforts of the psychiatric profession to have patients with serious mental illness treated in the general hospital began to meet with success. By the early 1970s one general hospital in every five had a separate inpatient psychiatric unit and an equal number accepted psychiatric patients for treatment on their regular medical or surgical wards. Counting only the larger general hospitals (500 beds or more), more than 75 percent now have inpatient psychiatric services. General hospitals are, as a rule, well staffed and equipped and are able to provide adequate psychiatric treatment. Since psychiatric service in a general hospital is essentially short-term care (a few days to a few weeks), patients who do not recover within a short period are discharged and referred to another hospital for extended care and treatment. The transfer is generally to a state mental hospital or to a VA neuropsychiatric hospital.

Admission to the psychiatric service of a general hospital is entirely voluntary, as it is for any other hospital medical or surgical service.

Many general hospitals have added outpatient psychiatric clinics, and some have 24-hour emergency psychiatric service.

The psychiatric services in some general hospitals have

introduced "day hospital" and "night hospital" care. Many psychiatric patients do not need to be in a hospital 24 hours a day. Day hospital treatment permits them to come to the hospital in the morning and go home at night. Night hospital care permits them to work or go to school during the day and come to the hospital for treatment at night, staying overnight.

The State Mental Hospital

Up to the early 1950s, the only places a person with serious mental illness could go for treatment were a state mental hospital, a Veterans mental hospital, or—for those who could afford it—a small private mental hospital.

As general hospitals began to open psychiatric sections, many patients with serious mental illness began to go there for treatment, instead of to the state hospital. In recent years the number of admissions to the psychiatric sections of the general hospitals has been as high as the total admission of the state mental hospitals. However, the general hospital can take only patients requiring short-term care.

The state mental hospitals continue to admit patients requiring both short-term and long-term care. A program of intensive treatment for patients on admission now enables most of these hospitals to discharge the majority of their admissions within a few months. Those who do not respond to existing treatment methods become chronic or long-term-care patients. As a result, the state mental hospitals house an accumulation of hundreds of thousands of mental patients for whom, under existing conditions, the prognosis is poor. Prognosis is to a great extent dependent on the ability of the hospitals to give continued intensive treatment. Most state mental hospitals are grossly understaffed and can therefore give intensive treatment only to patients on admission. Were they able to continue intensive treatment for longer periods and extend it to chronic patients, many more of their patients could be discharged with partial or even total recovery.

Most state mental hospitals consist of a group of buildings situated away from the community and housing between 1,500 and 5,000 patients. The current goal is for much smaller hospitals located in the community.

On admission, the state mental hospital patient is generally given an intensive course of treatment, including, as appropriate, drug therapy, electroshock, group psychotherapy, and in some rare instances, individual psychotherapy. In addition, there are recreational and occupational therapy programs. Attempts are made to keep the patients active and interested and in contact with the outside world through the visits of volunteers and relatives and through visits of patients to the community.

Because of staff shortages, the average state mental hospital has only one doctor to every 100 patients; some as few as one to 250 patients. In the admission wards, the doctor-patient ratio is better, averaging about one doctor for every 50 patients.

The psychiatric nurse is largely responsible for the medical supervision of the patient, under the direction of the doctor. A key member of the staff is the psychiatric aide (or attendant), who is in constant attendance to help the doctor and nurse and to assist the patient with his personal needs. Most patients in state mental hospitals are housed on wards or in cottages with between 25 to 100 beds. Some have smaller wards and many have individual rooms for one, two, and three patients.

Only one in every three state mental hospitals has facilities for the treatment of mentally ill children. Those that do may either house the children on the same ward as the adult patients or may have children's units. A children's unit may consist of one or more cottages set aside for children, or it may consist of a wing or ward of a building in which other patients are also housed. A few state hospitals emphasize schooling for their child patients and bring in teachers especially equipped for this work. Most have no educational program at all.

Because of the effectiveness of the psychiatric drugs, improvements in staffing, and concentration of treatment for patients on admission, many state mental hospitals are now able to discharge up to 85 percent of their patients within about three months after admission. Some of the patients can remain well without further treatment. Others need to have follow-up treatment with psychiatric drugs for several months, or even for several years. Many of the state mental hospitals have set up outpatient follow-up clinics in the community, staffed by hospital personnel. In some instances, the clinics are located in rehabilitation centers which also provide social and vocational rehabilitation services.

Since admission to a state mental hospital may involve loss of liberty during time of treatment, the terms under which a patient is admitted and the manner in which this is done becomes quite important. There are four ways in which a patient may be admitted to a mental hospital:

Informal admission. The patient merely applies at the hospital and says he wants help. No papers are signed. The patient may leave at will. Not many states have this type of admission.

Voluntary admission. In voluntary admission, the patient comes to the hospital, says he is sick and needs treatment, and signs a paper asking for hospitalization and treatment. He may leave at any time provided he gives the hospital several days notice of his intention to leave (customarily 3 to

10 days). Many states have voluntary admission. Many do not, requiring commitment.

Medical certification. Medical certification is a form of commitment. A relative comes to a doctor and says he believes a member of his family is mentally sick and in need of hospitalization. The doctor then examines the patient, and if in his judgment the patient should be hospitalized, he signs a certificate to that effect. (In some states, two doctors are required for medical certification.) The relative then takes the patient to the hospital and presents him for admission, together with the medical certification. It is not always necessary for the certifying doctor to be an "outside" doctor. A relative may bring the patient to a hospital and state that the patient is sick and in need of treatment. The examination will then be made by the hospital admitting doctor, and, if it is his judgment that the patient should be hospitalized, he will issue medical certification for commitment.

Sometimes it will not be a relative, but a law enforcement officer who will request medical certification.

A relative confronted by a member of the family who becomes suddenly agitated, destructive, or even violent, may call the police. They, in turn, may bring the patient before a private doctor or a doctor in a general hospital for examination and medical certification. Or else they may bring him to the mental hospital and there ask for certification by the admitting physician.

Legal or judicial commitment. In legal commitment, the patient is taken before a judge for a sanity hearing. He may be brought there on the petition of a relative, a law enforcement official, or a medical doctor. The judge hears testimony on the necessity for hospitalization and treatment. He will have a doctor present to advise him. Sometimes this doctor is a psychiatrist. Often he is not. Relatives or others may be present to offer testimony for or against commitment. The judge then decides to make judicial commitment or to release the patient.

In some states, all four forms of admission are used. Some states will not permit informal or voluntary admission, but will require medical certification or judicial commitment. Some will permit only judicial commitment.

A patient who is committed is under hospital jurisdiction, indefinitely, until the hospital decides that he is sufficiently recovered to leave. In some states medical certification alone has the full force of requiring indefinite commitment. In others it has only the force of holding the patient in the hospital until the certification is endorsed by a judge or until a judicial commitment hearing can be held.

Regardless of the procedure by which a patient is admitted to a state mental hospital, there are unbreachable legal safeguards to assure that no patient may be subjected to forced commitment against his personal interests or rights. All admission and commitment proceedings are buttressed by the regular state and federal constitutional guarantees against deprivation of liberty without due process of law. Beyond that is the fact that mental hospital authorities, motivated by medical, humanitarian, and practical considerations, are much more anxious to get patients out than keep them in.

Veterans Administration Mental Hospitals

Veterans with service-connected mental disorders are eligible for treatment in Veterans Administration mental hospitals. Veterans with mental illness which is not service-connected may be admitted if the patient is indigent and if there is room. There are about sixty VA mental hospitals in the United States. They give the same types of treatment as the state mental hospitals, but, because they are more fully staffed and better equipped, they are able to provide more thorough and adequate treatment than the state hospitals.

Private Mental Hospitals

There are several hundred private mental hospitals in the United States, with the number of beds ranging from fifty to five hundred. These operate like any other private hospital but take only psychiatric patients. Some will take only certain kinds of cases; others will take any case of mental illness. Admission is voluntary (although in some states, commitment may be required). These hospitals give drug treatment, shock, group therapy, and individual therapy. Some are operated by religious institutions or philanthropic organizations, and their fees are accordingly moderate. Others are proprietary (operated for profit) and their fees are much higher. Most private mental hospitals concentrate to a much greater degree on psychotherapy than the state mental hospitals and general hospitals are able to do.

Treatment Services for Children

There are still very few special facilities for the treatment of children with severe emotional disturbance and mental illness. Those in existence can care for only a very small fraction of the hundreds of thousands who need such services.

One type of facility for emotionally disturbed and mentally ill children is the residential treatment center. This is a small facility, taking care of between ten and fifty children (a few run higher) and combining the features of a home, a hospital, and a school. Residential treatment centers are for children who are so disturbed that it is impossible or extremely difficult for them to function at home and in school, even with psychiatric treatment. They need long-term care and the protected environment of a residential center.

In the residential treatment center, the children receive various forms of psychotherapy and in some cases psychiatric drugs. The psychotherapy is largely supportive and educational, aimed at removing the child's bewilderment and his fear and mistrust of his surroundings. He is helped to develop warm, trusting relationships with the psychiatrist, social worker, psychologist, nurse, teacher, and other personnel who take care of him, and eventually with other people in the world outside. He also is given schooling specially adapted to his condition and needs.

Some children improve greatly under this treatment, being freed of their most severe symptoms and being enabled to carry on a nearly normal life. Others are so sick that even this type of special, intensive treatment cannot do more than relieve them of some of their major symptoms. Under any circumstances, the treatment of mentally ill children is a long, difficult process.

Another facility for the treatment of severely disturbed children is the day care center or day school. Here the children receive much the same kind of treatment and schooling given in the residential treatment center. A major difference is that in the day center or day school, the children go home in the afternoon and come back again the following morning.

The Community Mental Health Center

Traditionally, the mentally ill have been treated in remote institutions away from the community. The result has been to separate the patient from personal ties in the community and to keep treatment and care of the patient isolated from the many medical and social services existing in the community. Isolation of the mental institution from the community's medical schools, hospitals, and university research centers has kept out the influence of modern developments in psychiatry and sealed in many antiquated treatment practices. One purpose of the community mental health center is to bring the treatment of the mentally ill into the mainstream of modern treatment practice—to include them in the community.

Another is to provide adequate and coordinated services. Facilities for the treatment of the different types of mental illnesses and different groups of patients have emerged, over the years, in a haphazard fashion. The result has been a patchwork of services, uneven, scattered, inadequate, and uncoordinated.

The mental health center provides a comprehensive range of services for all types of mental illness, for all ages, and for all stages of illness, from diagnosis through treatment and rehabilitation; it also connects these services functionally, either by bringing them under one roof or by bringing them together in a coordinated network.

Ideally, a mental health center should provide care and treatment for the psychoses, the neuroses, the personality disorders, and alcoholism; its services should also include suicide prevention and crisis intervention. It should serve children and adults and should provide the various types of psychotherapy and physical therapy. It should provide diagnosis, outpatient (clinic) treatment, inpatient (hospital) treatment, 24-hour emergency service, part-time hospitalization (day hospital and night hospital care), and rehabilitation service for improved or recovered patients after their discharge from treatment.

Keeping these services tied together in a functional network provides the patient with continuity of care. As his condition changes and his treatment and rehabilitation requirements change, he is referred from one service in the center to another as required, instead of being left to his own resources to find whatever other help he needs.

There are still not very many community health centers in the United States (perhaps 500 to 1,000), and only a small proportion provide a complete range of services, but the number is increasing, and those that exist continue to improve and expand.

CHAPTER TEN

Getting Help

The earlier a mentally sick person gets treatment the better are his chances for recovery. Because many mental illnesses drag on without acute, sharply disturbing episodes, there is a tendency to do nothing about them—especially when the patient or his relatives do not know what to do. As with physical illness, delay in getting help makes the illness more difficult to treat and cure.

Decades ago there might have been some excuse for this reluctance, because there was little that could be done for most mental illness and the only place a patient could be sent was to an "asylum." But this is no longer the case. There are many different kinds of treatment for the different mental illnesses, and there are any number of different kinds of inpatient and outpatient facilities; even in the state mental hospital a patient can get at least basic psychiatric treatment on admission and for several months thereafter.

Private psychiatrists and psychiatric clinics report that most of the patients they treat for neurosis are relieved of their most difficult symptoms and are able to lead more satisfying and productive lives.

The hospitals report high rates of improvement and recovery for most of the prevalent psychoses—schizophrenia, manic-depressive psychosis, involutional psychosis, and psychotic depressive reaction. With the use of psychiatric drugs, shock therapy, individual psychotherapy, and group therapy, the hospitals (state mental hospitals, veterans hospitals, general hospitals, private hospitals) are able to discharge between 65 percent and 85 percent of the patients suffering from these illnesses within a few weeks to a few months after admission. While many of the discharged patients are apt to suffer a relapse, the relapse rate can be held to about 10 percent through the intensive use of follow-up medical care (drugs) and rehabilitation services which help the patient to make a social and occupational readjustment.

Even the psychoses of old age are responding with unexpected success to modern treatment methods, especially the psychiatric drugs. Until recently it had been assumed that very little could be done for patients with senile psychosis and psychosis with cerebral arteriosclerosis, because of the belief that there was brain deterioration in these illnesses. This view has changed considerably with the recent disclosure that many of these patients do respond to treatment, some sufficiently to permit their return to home and community and even to holding a job.

To get help for mental illness—any kind of mental illness—the patient should go to see a doctor. If he cannot act for himself, his family should call the doctor or take the patient to see him.

If the patient is suffering from a serious mental illness, the doctor will be able to examine him and get him started on the next steps for the necessary treatment. If the symptoms are extreme and severe (like acute agitation, depression, derangement, unruly behavior), the doctor may decide that the patient needs to go to a hospital. If there is a general hospital with psychiatric service in the community, the doctor may refer him there for treatment. If not, or if the doctor should think that the patient's condition warrants it, he will recommend admission to a mental hospital, and then help the family to make the necessary arrangements. He may call the hospital himself, or tell the family whom to call and what to say. He will explain to the family the different regulations concerning voluntary admission and medical or judicial commitment. He may go with the patient and the family to the hospital. If the patient should need it, he will be able, in the meantime, to give the patient a psychiatric drug as a temporary measure.

If the doctor does not think that the patient needs to be hospitalized, he may refer him to a private psychiatrist or to an outpatient psychiatric clinic.

If there is any doubt in the doctor's mind, he will call in a psychiatrist for consultation or refer the patient directly to a psychiatrist for further examination, diagnosis, and decision as to treatment.

Sometimes the doctor will himself accept the patient for treatment. In areas where there is a shortage of psychiatrists, nonpsychiatric medical doctors have worked out arrangements to treat psychiatric patients in consultation with a psychiatrist.

The patient (or family) may wish to go to a psychiatrist, in the first instance, rather than to the family doctor (as they might wish to go to a specialist directly, in the case of any other serious illness). They would be wise, then, to ask the family doctor for some suggestions as to a psychiatrist. If he does not know of any, he can obtain the information for the family from the district branch of the American Psychiatric Association. That organization will have a directory of all APA members living and practicing in the city and information on medical training, postgraduate training, residency, clinical positions held, teaching and research positions held, and other background information. On the basis of this information the family, with the guidance of the family doctor, can make a choice.

In emergency situations, when there is not time enough to get a doctor—situations in which the patient is extremely agitated, destructive, violent, or suicidal—the police should be called. The officer on the phone should be told that help is needed with a mentally sick person who is out of control. Relatives need have little fear about mistreatment of the patient by police. Most police departments have, with the assistance of their mental health associations, given their police officers training in the proper handling of mentally sick people. There are certain fundamental facts these officers will know, and others who might have occasion to deal with highly disturbed mental patients should know them, too:

A patient is violent because he is terribly frightened by imaginary enemies, voices, or hallucinations. He will not see the members of his family realistically. He thinks they, too, are the enemy and he will fight them.

The agitation, disturbance, and violence come in bursts and will tend to wear themselves out.

The agitated, disturbed patient should not be threatened, bullied, scolded, or hit.

A calm, unthreatening, yet firm and authoritative approach will in most cases quiet the disturbed patient, and quickly.

In a small percentage of cases, force may need to be used

to restrain the patient. If so, it should be done by people who know how to do it without injuring the patient or themselves, such as hospital personnel or police. Very often, just surrounding the patient will bring willing submission.

However much the patient may appear to be out of contact, he will generally hear, know, and understand a great deal of what is going on around him. Things should therefore not be said or done in his presence which would degrade him or belittle him.

Never lie to a patient. He should be told he is sick, in need of treatment, that the police (or hospital personnel) are here to take him to the mental hospital for treatment, and that a member of the family will go along. If the patient is deceived and tricked into coming to the hospital, he will resent it bitterly, and the resentment may not only interfere with treatment but actually prevent recovery.

Often there is more resistance from the family than from the patient. This is understandable. The wife or husband or parents think of the relative going into an "insane asylum" with all those "crazy" people, and they are upset about how the patient will react. Actually, they are projecting their own feelings into the situation. This is how they, as normal people, would feel. They do not realize that the patient's feelings are, at this point, not like their own. If the patient is in a confused and agitated state, his surroundings will make very little difference. But even after he quiets down and becomes aware of his surroundings, he is very likely to experience a feeling of kinship with the other patients and to develop a human, warm, friendly, and protective feeling toward them.

While the dullness, routine, and inactivity of the mental hospital may be distressing to the relative, it may be a welcome relief (in the first days or weeks, at least) to the patient as compared with the disturbing, distressing situation from which he has just come. In the hospital he does not need to respond or react except on a very simple and elementary level. He can leave others alone and they will leave him alone.

In a case involving a seriously disturbing life problem (a marriage problem, job problem, family conflict, adoption, divorce), the doctor may suggest a family service agency where social case work could be done in the problem situation. Or else the patient (or family) could go directly to the family service agency. Many of these agencies have psychiatric clinics and can provide this additional service if it is required.

If the patient or family wishes first to become acquainted with all the different psychiatric, social welfare, and public health facilities and services in a community, they can obtain this information from the local mental health association. Most mental health associations affiliated with the National Association for Mental Health provide this service both through a printed directory and through personal consultation.

Index

Index

schizophrenia (*cont.*)
  hebephrenic, 40–41
  onset of, 38–39
  paranoid, 41–42, 49
  simple, 40
senile psychosis, 47–48, 86, 87, 109
sense of time and place, loss of, 53
seratonin, 88
Serax, 87
sexual frigidity, 74
sexual interest, decline of, 46
sexual relations, difficulty in, 29, 54
shock therapy, 89, 94, 104, 109
Sinequan, 87
sleepwalking, 34
social case work, 97
social factors in mental illness, 18
social worker, psychiatric, 92–93, 95, 96, 104
sociopath, 71
somatotherapy, 75
somnambulism, 34
Sparine, 53
"split" personality, 37
starvation, self-, 62–63
state mental hospitals, 98, 99–103
Stelazine, 53, 86
stomach cramps, 61
stomach ulcers, 59–60
stubbornness, 70
suicide, 45, 46, 47, 69, 79, 86, 111
supportive psychotherapy, 79–80, 95, 105
suspiciousness, 25, 38, 48, 53, 71, 88
swallowing, difficulty in, 29
symbiotic child, 43–44
syphilis, 16, 20

tantrums, 27
taste, loss of, 33
tension:
  emotional, 29, 64, 68, 87
  muscular, 56
  neurotic, 87
thioridazine, 53, 86
thiothixene, 86
Thorazine, 53, 86
thoughts:
  delusional, 37
  disorganized, 40–41
  obssessive, 32
  preoccupation with, 38
  repressed, 76
Three Faces of Eve, 35
tic, 26
Tofranil, 87
toilet training, 23
tranquilizers, 53, 55, 86–88
transference, 77, 81
tranylcypromene, 87
trifluoperazine, 53, 86, 87
triflupromazine, 53
trigger amines, 88
Trilafon, 86
twitch, uncontrollable, 33

ulcers, 57, 59–61
urinary frequency, 64

Valium, 87
vascular hypertension, 58
Veterans Administration mental hospitals, 98, 99, 103–104
vector therapy, 82
Vesprin, 53
violence, 48, 71, 111
violent patient, handling of, 111–12
vitamin metabolism, interference of alcohol with, 53–54

ABOUT THE AUTHOR

Harry Milt was for fourteen years director of public information for the National Association for Mental Health; he is now coordinator of the anti-smoking program of the American Cancer Society. Mr. Milt is also the author of *Basic Handbook on Alcoholism* and of monographs on delinquency and suicide for the National Institute of Mental Health and co-author with George S. Stevenson, M.D., of *Master Your Tensions and Enjoy Living Again.*